SWINGING FRENCH JAZZ

BISTRO

FAVORITE PARISIAN BISTRO RECIPES

BOOKS IN THE MENUS AND MUSIC SERIES

Dinner and Dessert

Holidays

Dinners for Two

Nutcracker Sweet

Music and Food of Spain

Picnics

Dining and the Opera in Manhattan

Lighthearted Gourmet

Rock & Roll Diner

The Irish Isle

Afternoon Tea Serenade

Spa

Bistro

SWINGING FRENCH JAZZ

BISTRO

FAVORITE PARISIAN BISTRO RECIPES

by

SHARON O'CONNOR

assisted by

SARAH CREIDER

Menus and Music Productions, Inc.
Emeryville, California

Chez Pauline recipes adapted with permission by authors André Génin and Jean-Claude Colau from *La cuisine de Pauline: des recettes trois etoiles pour Pauline, trois ans* (published by First Editions, Paris, 1997).

Printed in Korea

Library of Congress Catalog Card Number: 99-070606

O'Connor, Sharon
Menus and Music Volume XIV
Bistro

  Swinging French Jazz
  Favorite Parisian Bistro Recipes

Includes Index
1. Cookery 2. Entertaining
I. Title

ISBN 1-883914-28-0 (paperback with music compact disc)

Menus and Music Productions, Inc.
1462 66th Street
Emeryville, CA 94608
(510) 658-9100
Web Site: www.menusandmusic.com

Book and cover design: Fifth Street Design, Berkeley, CA
Food photographer: Paul Moore
Food stylist: Amy Nathan
Prop stylist: Sara Slavin

10 9 8 7 6 5 4 3 2 1

CONTENTS

INTRODUCTION

To say I'm hopelessly smitten isn't even the half of it. In search of authentic recipes, I find myself hungry and in Paris at the same time! And for weeks, neighborhood streets have led me to the world of Parisian bistros. Joyous long lunches; cooking demonstrations in closet-sized bistro kitchens; romantic late-evening dinners; conversations with chefs, proprietors, and previous proprietors; recollections about running a bistro during the war and reminders of how much the French admire us Americans; astute questions about the American stock exchange; photo sessions in kitchens with *plats du jour* and soufflés in full swing; descents by steep stone stairways into underground caves housing everyday wines along with those of the previous century; answers to how the bistro got its name attached to brief history lessons; warm welcomes of kisses on three cheeks. My research for this volume has been the experience of a lifetime!

I'll always remember a party during the lull between lunch and dinner when I had the sudden realization that the hard-working bistro chef, his gracious, generous wife, and their fish, produce, and wine suppliers were, above all, steadfast friends celebrating life together; the dinner at an elegant bistro when I had a moment of panic about the correct way to use my flat, sauce spoon; a chef with good sense and integrity emerging from a late-night kitchen to make sure I had a certain cooking technique right; a lecture about crème fraîche and the importance of best-quality ingredients in creating dishes of memorable flavor; the animated connection between proprietors and their regulars; a fashionable bistro owner of acrobatic agility carrying abundant plates from the kitchen to a small ancient room of urbane, hungry patrons—and the look of contentment that was soon on everyone's face; meals that were utterly satisfying.

Bistros have met the exacting standards of Parisians in their daily appreciation of good food and good value for nearly two centuries. Bistro cooking isn't haute cuisine or nouvelle cuisine, but although it is less complicated food, it is certainly no less delicious. The recipes included here have pleased diners throughout Paris, and now you can serve the same satisfying food at home. In this cookbook, twenty talented chefs, each with his or her own style, provide you with authenic bistro recipes and an introduction to the rich tradition of French cuisine. Some of my favorites are French Onion Soup (page 196), Grilled Turbot with White Butter Sauce (page 130), Cauliflower au Gratin (page 78), Citrus Terrine with Orange Coulis (page 52), and Tarte Tatin (page 187).

These recipes are perfectly suited to the home cook, and many are ideal for entertaining since they can be made in advance—in fact most taste even better the next day. I've found that the veal stew or coq au vin I make over the weekend tastes even more delicious when served as a Monday-night dinner. You'll find dishes that feed a crowd easily, dishes that you can put on the stove and all but forget, and dishes that can be cooked very quickly. You don't need to be a highly skilled chef to prepare any of these recipes, and you won't need a collection of fancy pots and pans or a large kitchen equiped with many appliances. In fact, the kitchens of most of the chefs in this book are astonishingly small and basic, and most of the chefs, like most home cooks, emphasize simplicity.

Recipes are really only a guideline and source of inspiration for great home cooking. So, add or subtract ingredients according to your taste or according to seasonal availability—this type of improvising makes cooking fun. If you are trying to minimize the fat in your diet, you can reduce the amount of butter by half in many of these recipes without noticing much change in taste or texture. Some of these bistro dishes may remind you of your Mom's home-cooked meals. For instance, American beef stew and macaroni and cheese bears a striking resemblance to Estouffade and Macaroni au Parmesan (page 208). And the rice pudding we remember from childhood is found here with a caramelized topping, a delicious French touch.

The spririted jazz that was recorded for this volume sets a Parisian mood for dining, cooking, and relaxing after wonderful meals. The city of Django Reinhardt and Stephane Grappelli holds sway in the intangible realms of style and romance, and a soulful ballad like "Autumn Leaves" puts you under its spell, while "Under Paris Skies" captures an atmospheric moment that touches the heart and immediately transports you to Paris. The energy of tunes like "Sweet Georgia Brown" and "Them There Eyes" conjure up images of crowded Parisian bistros and confirm that some styles are timeless. It was a dream come true for me to record the top New York- and Miami-based jazz musicians that you hear on this compact disc. Not only are they highly skilled, they possess the rare gift of prodigious musical talent. These brilliant players are at the top of their game, and their performances bring us the nuance and genius of a previous generation of musicians—they carry tradition forward for us to enjoy. I hope you'll be able to hear the tremendous amount of fun everyone had during the recording sessions!

When dining out, it is no longer necessary to travel to France in order to enjoy bistro cuisine. The immense popularity of New York's Balthazar and California's Bouchon are testament to the widespread hunger for French bistro cuisine on both sides of the Atlantic. In order to enjoy the world of Parisian bistros, plan a visit to the dazzling City of Light and experience the pleasure for yourself. In the meantime, I hope this volume helps you to create many delicious meals and plays a part in your enjoyment of bistro-style dining at home. *Bon appétit!*

—*Sharon O'Connor*

BISTRO HISTORY

The rustic, unpretentious atmosphere associated with Parisian bistros reflects their origins. Most of the first bistros started out as *cafés-charbons*, shops that sold coal and firewood for heating, where neighbors could meet for a glass of wine or cup of coffee. When the owners of these simple wine bars, usually workers from the Auvergne region in central France, began to offer a few modest dishes served family style to their guests, the bistro tradition was born. These first bistros were places for working people to eat quickly around Les Halles, the historic market district of Paris. By the mid-1800s, neighborhood bistros had popped up in almost every district of the city. Along with the laborers came artists and intellectuals, attracted by delicious, inexpensive meals.

For Parisians who lived in apartments with limited or nonexistent kitchens, the closest thing to a home-cooked meal could be found at neighborhood bistros. And because the same patrons returned night after night, these restaurants offered more than old-fashioned country cuisine—they were also places where Parisians could escape the anonymity of the big city. In France, bistro cuisine is often called *cuisine de grand-mère*. The simple salads and steaks, braised stews and meats, and comforting, homespun desserts served in most bistros are the kinds of dishes you would expect to be served by a French grandmother.

⊰ BISTRO ⊱

There are several theories about the origins of the word *bistro*. The most picturesque story traces the word back to the Russian soldiers who marched into Paris after Napolean's defeat at Waterloo in 1815. Legend has it that the hungry soldiers dashed into the city's wine-shops and cafés, shouting *"Bistro! bistro!"*—Russian for "Quiek! quick!" Other sources suggest that the word was derived from *bistouille*, slang for a mixture of eau-de-vie and coffee, which was served in early cafés.

BISTROS TODAY

Just a few years ago, many Parisians were worried that their beloved neighborhood bistros would soon be an endangered species. The popularity of *nouvelle cuisine*, an invasion of American-style fast food, and rising costs in Paris have indeed caused some old favorites to close their doors. But recently, bistros have become chic once again. In fact, some of Paris's most famous restaurateurs have opened bistro-style restaurants. As well, many up-and-coming chefs are serving their own innovative cuisine to a local clientele at small, casual establishments. And there are still plenty of traditional bistros in Paris, where generous portions of French comfort food are served in an unpretentious atmosphere.

BRASSERIES AND CAFÉS

When Parisians are looking for traditional fare in a casual atmosphere, they can choose between a bistro, a brasserie, and a café. Although the lines between the three types of establishments can be blurry, there are still some differences in style, atmosphere, and cuisine.

Brasserie

Most brasseries were founded by Alsatians who came to Paris after the Franco-Prussian war. Their Germanic influence can be seen in the popularity of beer as opposed to wine (*brasserie* means brewery in French) and in hearty one-dish meals like *choucroute garnie*: sauerkraut served with various kinds of pork and sausages. Bright and cheerful, with lots of floor space and high ceilings, brasseries are often open late at night.

Café

The most important characteristic of a Parisian café is that it is designed for long hours spent lingering over nothing more than a *café express*. If bistros are all about food, cafés are for chatting, reading newspapers, or simply watching pedestrians go by. Not all cafés serve meals, and those that do usually offer a very limited menu. Sandwiches, salads, and perhaps one *plat du jour* are typical.

ARRONDISSEMENTS

Paris is divided into twenty numbered sections, or *arrondissements*, which spiral out from the center of the city. When you ask where a restaurant or monument is located in Paris, the answer is often based on arrondissement rather than neighborhood: "Have you been to the market at place Maubert-Mutualité in the fifth?" or "I know the greatest bistro in the tenth!" The zip codes in Paris are based on arrondissement. A bistro with a 75001 zip code is in the first arrondissement, while one in the eighth has a 75008 zip code.

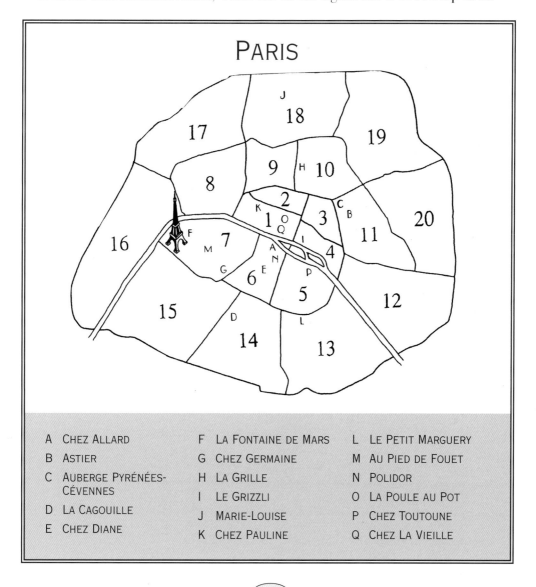

PARIS

A Chez Allard	F La Fontaine de Mars	L Le Petit Marguery
B Astier	G Chez Germaine	M Au Pied de Fouet
C Auberge Pyrénées-Cévennes	H La Grille	N Polidor
	I Le Grizzli	O La Poule au Pot
D La Cagouille	J Marie-Louise	P Chez Toutoune
E Chez Diane	K Chez Pauline	Q Chez La Vieille

WHAT TO EXPECT AT A PARISIAN BISTRO

A closed door can be one of the greatest pleasures of traveling. There's nothing like standing in front of an unknown building in a foreign city, about to enter a new and mysterious world. Who knows what's waiting behind that imposing nineteenth-century door? And what about the door with an etched-glass window and lace curtains tucked away on a quiet street? If you're visiting a Paris bistro, you might find a tiny room with mustard-colored walls and just a handful of paper-covered tables—or a narrow, elegant space with burgundy velvet banquettes, huge vases of flowers, and beautiful antique mirrors. Either way, when you open the door, you'll probably be greeted like an old friend.

Dining at a bistro is almost like an invitation into a French home. The atmosphere of each establishment reflects the style, taste, and background of its proprietor. Even the decor is often personalized, with posters, lamps, and other treasures from the owner's private collection.

Reservations and Seating

Although bistros are casual restaurants, French society as a whole is more formal than American. For the evening meal, a reservation is almost always necessary, and it's expected that you will arrive on time.

However, part of the bistro tradition is a friendly, convivial atmosphere where fellow diners become friends by the end of a meal, and even with a reservation you may find yourself sharing a table. Solitary diners are sometimes seated next to complete strangers, wherever there's an extra chair. Groups may also enjoy the pleasure of unexpected dining companions— many bistros seat their guests "elbow to elbow," as they say in France, at a long row of tables in the middle of the dining room.

Ordering

Once you've been seated, your waiter will ask if you'd like an aperitif, or before-dinner drink. While sipping a glass of wine or perhaps a Kir (white wine with a dash of black currant liqueur), you can peruse the menu.

In most cases, you'll have a choice between two styles of ordering—a *menu prix fixe* or *à la carte*. Carte means menu in French, and to order *à la carte* is simply to order from the menu, as you would in any American restaurant. A *menu* (sometimes also called a *formule*) is a meal consisting of two or three courses at a set price, with a few choices per course. If you're on a budget, the *menu* is usually a good option.

Whether it's written on a blackboard, handwritten in the menu, or simply announced by the waiter, bistro habitués know that the plat du jour, or dish of the day, is delicious and usually based on seasonal ingredients.

Bread, Wine, and Water

For the French, no meal is complete without bread. A piece of baguette or slice of crusty bread is your trusty companion from appetizer to cheese course. It's perfectly polite to use your bread to sop up some of the delicious sauce on your plate, even in formal settings. But only in Normandy, the region in northern France famous for its dairy products, do the French spread butter on their baguette at mealtimes.

Wine can be ordered by the bottle, half bottle, or glass. In more casual bistros, the house wine also comes in a *pichet*, or small pitcher. If you're ordering from a menu prix fixe, *boisson compris* usually means that a *pichet* of house wine is included in the price of your meal. You can also order *une carafe d'eau*, or pitcher of tap water. For mineral water, ask for *une bouteille d'eau*, either *gazeuse* or *non-gazeuse:* with or without carbonation.

The Bill

When you're ready to leave, ask for *"l'addition, s'il vous plaît."* Tipping is never necessary, since a service charge is always included in the price of your meal. Waiting tables is taken seriously as a vocation in France, and waiters receive a salary rather than relying on tips to augment their wages.

Dining Hours

It is traditional in France for the principal meal of the day to be served in the early afternoon. Although many modern Parisians only have time for a quick midday sandwich, bistros still offer full meals at both lunch and dinner. In general, lunch is served between noon and 2 pm, and dinner from 8 to 10 at night. However, if you arrive at a bistro punctually at eight, don't be surprised if most of the tables are empty—within an hour, most likely the restaurant will be bustling with activity.

Almost all bistros are closed on Sundays. For family-run restaurants, at least one day of rest and recuperation is a necessity. Some places are also closed on Saturdays or Mondays. In addition, many bistros shut their doors for at least part of August and for the week between Christmas and New Year's.

The service at bistros is generally excellent, but even so, don't expect a quick meal. If you're in a hurry, grab a sandwich at a corner café and save your bistro experience for an afternoon or evening when you have a couple of hours free to devote to that extremely important pastime—enjoying your food. By the time you've chosen the perfect aperitif, appreciated your appetizer, chatted with the proprietor about the culinary differences between France and America, settled down with your main course, savored a wildly delicious dessert, and sipped on an espresso, you'll have forgotten there's any such thing as a schedule.

⊰ A TYPICAL BISTRO MEAL ⊱

COURSES

Whether you're preparing a bistro-style dinner at home or sitting down for lunch at your favorite bistro in Paris, here's a guide to a typical French meal, from start to finish.

APÉRITIF (BEFORE-DINNER DRINK)

The before-dinner drink is a fixture in France. A simple glass of wine, perhaps the one you'll enjoy with your first course, is always correct, and for special occasions there is always champagne. Also popular are Lillet, a wine-based drink from Bordeaux; pastis, an anise-flavored liqueur served with a pitcher of water for mixing; and Kir, white wine with a dash of black currant liqueur, or Kir royal, champagne mixed with crème de cassis. Some bistros have a special house aperitif, which is usually worth trying.

KIR

This drink is named after Canon Kir, a mayor of Dijon.

- 2 tablespoons crème de cassis
- 1 cup chilled dry white wine
- 2 lemon zest strips

Pour the crème de cassis into 2 stemmed glasses, add the wine, and gently stir to mix. Garnish with a twist of lemon zest.

Serves 2

ENTRÉE OR HORS D'OEUVRE (APPETIZER OR FIRST COURSE)

An *entrée* can be as simple as a slice of smoked ham or a few asparagus spears with vinaigrette dressing, or as complex as the Seafood Terrine on page 125. In a restaurant, salads are considered an appetizer, but they're often served at the end of a home-cooked meal. Classic bistro *entrées* include *oeufs en meurette*, eggs poached in red wine, and *salade composée*, assorted cold vegetables and salads dressed with vinaigrette.

PLAT (ENTRÉE)

The main course of a French meal almost always involves meat, chicken, or seafood. If you order one of the delicious cuts of steak popular at bistros, your waiter will ask how you like your meat. The typical Parisian likes his or her steak cooked *bleu*, or blue—seared on the outside and raw on the inside. For rare, ask for *saignant*, medium is *à point*, and well done is *bien cuit*.

DESSERT (DESSERT)

Most bistro desserts are simple favorites like rice pudding, chocolate cake, or *crème caramel*. Simplest of all is plain yogurt or *fromage blanc* (a fresh, creamy cheese), sprinkled with granulated sugar. Diners may choose to forego the dessert course and finish their meal with a selection of cheeses.

FROMAGE (CHEESE)

Cheese is served as a separate course in France, either before or in place of dessert. Some bistros offer a small serving of two or three different cheeses on a plate, while others allow diners to choose from an extensive cheese platter.

CAFÉ (COFFEE)

"Voulez-vous un café?" is a question you'll hear at the end of almost every meal in France. For the French, *un café* is an espresso, or café express, with sugar cubes if you wish, but no cream or milk. Coffee is served after dessert or the cheese course.

BISTRO MENU GLOSSARY

La Carte / The Menu

A la carte: From the menu.

Menu prix fixe: A menu of two, three, or four courses, with a limited choice of dishes per course, at a set price. Sometimes also listed *formule*, or simply *le menu*.

Plat du jour: Daily special.

Specialité de la maison: House specialty (*maison* can also mean homemade).

Les Boissons / Drinks

Apéritif: Before-dinner drink.

Bière: Beer.

Bouteille: Bottle.

Café: Espresso, sometimes called *café express*.

Carte des vins: Wine list.

Eau minérale: Mineral water.

Infusion: Herb tea.

Jus de fruits: Fruit juices.

Pichet: Literally, a jug; refers to a pitcher of wine.

Verre: Glass.

Vin: Wine.

Thé: Tea.

Entrées/Hors d'Oeuvres / First Courses/Appetizers

Aïoli: Garlic mayonnaise.

Bisque: A substantial soup, usually of shellfish.

Bourride: An egg-based Mediterranean fish and shellfish soup, served with aïoli.

Céleri rémoulade: Grated celery root in a creamy dressing.

Champignons à la grecque: Mushrooms marinated in olive oil and lemon juice, "Greek style."

Charcuterie: Cold cuts, sausages, terrines, pâtés.

Cochonnailles: An assortment of pork sausages and pâtés.

Crudités: Raw vegetables.

Escargots: Snails.

Filets de hareng: Pickled herring.

Foie gras: The liver of a fattened goose or duck.

Huîtres: Oysters.

Jambon: Ham.

Moules: Mussels.

Oeuf mayonnaise: Hard-cooked eggs with mayonnaise.

Oeufs en meurette: Eggs poached in red wine.

Pâté: Spiced ground meat baked in a mold, served hot or cold.

Potage: Soup, usually puréed.

Salade frisée aux lardons: A salad of curly endive and small pieces of slab bacon.

Salade verte: Green salad.

Saucisson: A dried sausage.

Tapenade: A paste of black olives, anchovies, capers, olive oil, and lemon juice.

Tartare: Chopped raw beef, seasoned and garnished with raw egg, capers, chopped onion, and parsley.

Vinaigrette: Oil and vinegar dressing.

Les Plats / Main Dishes

Agneau: Lamb.

Andouille: Tripe sausage.

Beurre blanc: A sauce of butter and reduced vinegar, white wine, and shallots.

Blanc de volaille: Breast of chicken.

Blanquette de veau: Veal in a rich cream sauce.

Boeuf: Beef.

Boeuf à la mode: Beef marinated and braised in red wine, served with carrots, mushrooms, onions, and turnips.

Boeuf bourguignon: Beef stew with red wine, onion, bacon, and mushrooms.

Boeuf en daube: Braised beef stew.

Brandade: A warm garlicky purée of salt cod, cream or oil, and potatoes.

Canard: Duck.

Cassolette: A dish presented in a small casserole.

Cassoulet: A casserole of white beans with various meats such as sausage, duck, pork, lamb, and goose.

Choucroute: Sauerkraut

Choucroute garnie: A main dish of sauerkraut with sausages, bacon, and pork, served with potatoes.

Confit de canard: Duck preserved in its own fat.

Coq au vin: Chicken braised in red wine.

Coquilles Saint-Jacques: Sea scallops.

Frites: French fries.

Fruits de mer: Seafood.

Gibier: Game, such as pheasant, boar, and venison.

Gigot d'agneau: Leg of lamb.

Gratin: A crusty-topped dish; also the casserole dish in which a gratin is cooked.

Hachis: Minced or chopped meat or fish.

Haricots: Beans.

Homard: Lobster.

Lapin: Rabbit.

Morue: Salt cod.

Oie: Goose.

Pavé: Literally, a paving stone; usually refers to a thick beef steak.

Lentilles: Lentils.

Parmentier: A dish with potatoes.

Pipérade: A Basque dish of peppers, onions, tomatoes, and often scrambled eggs and ham.

Plateau de fruits de mer: A seafood platter, usually including oysters, clams, mussels, periwinkles, and crabs.

Poireaux: Leeks.

Poisson: Fish.

Poitrine: Breast of meat or poultry.

Pommes de terre: Potatoes.

Porc: Pork.

Pot-au-feu: Boiled beef and vegetables.

Poule: Chicken.

Quenelles: Dumplings, usually of puréed fish.

Ratatouille: A cooked dish of eggplant, zucchini, onions, tomatoes, peppers, garlic, and olive oil.

Riz: Rice.

Salé: Salted or savory.

Saumon: Salmon.

Sole meunière: Sole floured, fried, and served with lemon, parsley, and browned butter.

Tête de veau: A head of veal, poached in wine and spices and served boned and sliced.

Truffe: Truffle.

Vapeur (à la): Steamed.

Veau: Veal.

Viande: Meat.

Volaille: Poultry.

Les Desserts / Dessert

Baba au rhum: Sponge cake soaked in rum-flavored syrup.

Charlotte: A molded custard with ladyfingers.

Clafoutis: Traditional tart made with batter and fruit, usually sweet cherries.

Crème anglaise: Custard sauce.

Crème brûlée: Custard with a melted sugar topping.

Crème Chantilly: Sweetened whipped cream.

Crème fraîche: Lightly tangy thickened cream; used in sauces and as a topping for savory and sweet dishes.

Crème de marrons: Sweetened chestnut purée.

Fromage: Cheese.

Fromage blanc: A creamy low-fat cheese with the consistency of smooth cottage cheese.

Gâteau: Cake.

Génoise: Sponge cake.

Glace: Ice cream.

Ile flottante: Poached meringue floating in custard sauce.

Mille-feuille: Usually a cream-filled rectangle of puff pastry or a napoleon.

Mousse: A light, airy mixture containing eggs and cream.

Pâtisserie: Pasty; also a pastry shop.

Petits fours: Tiny cakes and pastries.

Pot de crème: An individual custard or mousselike dessert, often chocolate.

Sabayon: A sweet, whipped sauce of egg yolks, sugar, wine, and flavoring.

Tarte: An open-faced pie.

Tarte-Tatin: A caramelized upside-down apple tart.

BISTRO STYLE AT HOME

BISTRO CUISINE

In France, even the most casual meals are served in courses. For home cooks, this style of dining can make entertaining easy, since there's no need to have everything ready at once. Take your time between courses, allowing a few minutes for conversation, for refilling wineglasses, and for guests to enjoy the flavors of each scrumptious dish.

Start your guests off with an *apéritif* (before-dinner drink) and thin slices of *saucisson* (French salami). Then, whet their appetites with a simple salad or soup. For meals that are more of an occasion, a delicious starter like Le Petit Marguery's marinated salmon (page 163) or Le Grizzli's Green Lentil and White Bean Terrine (page 137) can be prepared in advance. For the main course, rather than carefully arranging each plate in the kitchen, bring the whole casserole to the table and allow your guests to help themselves. Following the main course, toss the salad at the table. Generous servings are a must for any bistro-style meal.

Dessert can be replaced with a cheese course. Arrange at least three varieties on a platter and try to include a semi-soft cheese, a goat cheese, and a blue. If you are unable to find French cheeses, simply choose a few of your own favorites. Take a small portion of each cheese and begin with the mild cheese before proceeding to the stronger varieties. Serve *fromage* at room temperature, with plenty of fresh bread.

At the end of your meal, serve small cups of espresso. An after-dinner liqueur such as Armagnac or Calvados (apple cider brandy from Normandy) is an especially nice French touch.

For calorie-conscious Americans, there's something a little shocking about a cuisine that includes wine with most meals and in which cream is almost a staple. And yet, the majority of bistro diners are noticeably slender and chic. If you ask the French, they'll insist their secrets are simple—never eat between meals, avoid fast food, use only the freshest ingredients, eat small portions, and make time for a truly satisfying lunch or dinner each day. But actually, most people in France don't spend a lot of time worrying about nutrition. They're too busy enjoying their food! For bistro meals at home, cook with the best-quality ingredients you can find, serve several courses so guests feel satisfied without overeating, and most of all, take pleasure in a delicious dinner served in the company of good friends.

SETTING A BISTRO TABLE

The bistro look is about comfort, generosity, and your own personal style. Simple china and silverware can be set off with a plain white tablecloth and napkins, or a collection of antique lace. Place a basket filled with slices of crusty bread or pieces of baguette on the table, along with bottles of wine and water, and perhaps a simple bouquet of fresh flowers. Writing your menu out by hand and making a copy for each guest is a nice touch.

More important than any single piece of furniture or tableware is the golden glow that illuminates most Parisian bistros. To create this cozy ambience in your own home, turn off the overhead lights and rely on small candles and table lamps. If you wish, add depth to the lighting scheme by hanging a few mirrors on your dining room walls.

⊰ BISTRO WINES ⊱

Simple, easy-drinking wines are just right for bistro cuisine. Ideally, wine matches the intensity of flavors in food, and there is a delightful harmony when you experience the perfect pairing of wine and food. If you use wine in cooking a dish, it always works well to drink the same wine with your meal. Of course, your own taste and experience determine your likes and dislikes, but it's a good idea to remain open-minded and keep trying unexpected wine and food combinations. If you have two or more wines during a meal, start with the lightest wine and end with the heaviest or most full-flavored. Most French don't drink hard liquor before meals, and few bistros have a full bar.

Favorite bistro red wines produced in France include Beaujolais; Côtes-du-Rhône, such as Hermitage and Châteauneuf-du-Pape; wines of the Loire, such as Sancerre, Chinon, Bourgueil, and Saumur-Champigny; Pinot Noir from Alsace; Côtes de Provence and Bandol from Provence; and the full-bodied wines of the Southwest, such as Cahors and Madiran. Typical bistro white wines include Muscadet, Sancerre, Chablis, Mâcon, Saint-Véran, Sauvignon de Touraine, and Pouilly-Fumé.

At Parisian bistros, wines are often purchased by the proprietor directly from the vineyard and listed as vins de propriétaire. In California's Napa Valley wine country, Bouchon (page 71) carries on this tradition by offering wine from local vintners, who often create special blends just for the bistro. To accompany their meals, Bouchon recommends American red wines that aren't overly tannic, such as Syrah, Cabernet Franc, and Zinfandel, and white wines such as American-produced Rhone varietals and Sauvignon Blanc.

BISTRO STYLE AT HOME

⊰ FRENCH CHEESES ⊱

Brebignal: A mild sheep's milk cheese made in the Pyrénées.

Brie: Perhaps the most well known of French cheeses, this semi-soft cow's milk cheese has a chewy edible rind and is shaped like a disk.

Camembert: Made in the Normandy region of France, Camembert resembles a smaller version of Brie and has a strong aroma, mild flavor, and velvety texture. Both Camembert and Brie should be cut into wedges, like a pie.

Cantal: One of the oldest French cheeses, *cantal* is semi-firm, with a nutty flavor.

Chèvre: A general term for goat's milk cheese. Tangy and spreadable, a *chèvre* often comes shaped like a miniature log and is sometimes rolled in herbs or spices.

Comté: Similar in flavor to Swiss Gruyère.

Crottins: Tiny buttons of dried *chèvre*, often preserved in olive oil.

Gruyère: Firm and dense, Gruyère is often used in gratins.

Reblochon: A semi-soft cheese with a smooth mild flavor made in the Savoie region of France.

Roquefort: France's most famous blue cheese, made from sheep's milk.

Vacherin: Best in the winter months, Vacherin is a creamy cow's milk cheese; the rind is removed before eating. During the aging process, the cheese is brushed with white wine, which gives it a wonderful, luxurious flavor.

BISTRO STYLE AT HOME

MUSIC NOTES

Having had the opportunity to work with great musicians like clarinetist Ken Peplowski, violinist Federico Ruiz, guitarists Frank Vignola and Mike Peters, bassist Michael Moore, and accordionist Charlie Giordano, I feel lucky indeed. Now that this recording is finished, we're all fortunate to hear their superb artistry.

"April in Paris," a song that is the very breath of romance, makes us yearn for the City of Light at any time of the year, but especially in spring-time. Composer Vernon Duke introduced it in the 1932 show *Walk a Little Faster*, and it became his first jazz standard.

Jacques Prevert and Joseph Kosma, who teamed up in the mid-1940s to create the script for the French film *Children of Paradise*, wrote "Autumn Leaves," a love song whose melody everyone knows. In France, *"Les Feuilles Mortes"* is closely associated with Yves Montand. Edith Piaf recorded the tune in English, but never in French.

"Flamingo," a tune that was often heard in the jazz clubs of Europe during the 1940s, was revived by Stephane Grappelli, the French master of the jazz violin who attained worldwide celebrity during the 1970s and 80s. Grappelli loved the tune so much that *Flamingo* is the title of his fine 1995 duet recording with jazz pianist Michael Petruciani.

"Swing 39" was written by guitarist Django Reinhardt and violinist Stephane Grappelli during their days together in the Quintet of the Hot Club of France, the group they co-founded in 1934. Until its dissolution at the outbreak of the war, the quintet was one of the most important jazz groups of the day.

Apart from Django Reinhardt's skill as a guitarist, he was a composer of distinction. On this recording we hear three of his best-remembered compositions, "Shine," "Nuages," and "Swing 42." "Nuages" is a langorously beautiful exploration of the whole tone scale, and "Swing 42" a tribute to Django's idol, Louis Armstrong. He created the song one evening while imitating Armstrong's vocal style. Recorded in 1941, it was one of the most popular tunes in Paris during the war.

"Sweet Georgia Brown" (1925) and "Them There Eyes" (1929), part of every jazzman's staple diet during the 1930s and 40s, are enduringly popular and heard here in performances full of wit and daring.

"La Vie en Rose" is the song most identified with the petite French chanteuse Edith Piaf, whose mercurial rise to fame and tragic life are legendary. On this recording we also hear two other enormous hits for Piaf, "Padam, Padam" and "De l'Autre Côté de la Rue," which was composed in 1942 by Michel Emer who also wrote "L'Accordéoniste," another important song for Piaf.

Henri Contet, composer of more than forty songs sung by Edith Piaf, wrote the classic "Under Paris Skies," a lilting melody that evokes the feeling of being in love under the city's moody skies.

"Fascinating Rhythm" is a George Gershwin tune from the 1924 musical *Lady Be Good!* The song was sung by Cliff "Ukelele Ike" Edwards, and in Gershwin's words, it was "followed by a miraculous dance by Fred and Adele Astaire." Fred Astaire credits Gershwin with conceiving the exit dance steps that nightly stopped the show.

CHEZ ALLARD

O nce home to Racine, the famous French poet and playwright, 41, rue St-André-des-Arts is one of many historic buildings in Paris's ancient Latin Quarter. In 1720, under royal ordinance, a wine merchant set up shop on the first floor, and over the course of the next two hundred years, the wine store evolved into a Paris institution of international fame: Chez Allard.

Monsieur and Madame Allard established their bistro in the early 1930s, and on retiring they handed the reins over to their son and daughter-in-law, André and Fernande. In most bistro kitchens the husband reigns supreme; however, at Allard the wives, Marthe and Fernande, created the famous specialties that remain on the menu today. Their recipes for Burgundian specialties such as Coq au Vin (page 35), *boeuf bourguignon*, and *canard aux olives* (duck with olives) are now made by chef Didier Remay, who cooked for twenty years under Fernande Allard. Fernande retired in 1985 but still lives in the family apartments above the bistro and is a frequent evening visitor.

Monsieur Layrac, the proprietor since 1995, has lavished considerable attention on Allard's cuisine and decor. Although he has spruced up the entire bistro, the original dining room has been kept almost perfectly intact. With a vintage zinc bar, pressed-tin ceiling, tile floors, mustard-colored walls, and lovely old prints, this room resembles a living bistro museum. On the other side of the busy open kitchen, a charming newer dining room is popular with regulars.

NEIGHBORHOOD WALK

From the Odéon métro station, a short walk down rue de l'Ancienne-Comédie leads to the carrefour de Buci, a gourmet haven. Besides a daily produce market, the plaza boasts tea salons, patisseries, restaurants, and shops that sell everything from flowers to roasted chicken. From Buci, you can turn down rue St-André-des-Arts towards the Latin Quarter, or simply wander through the small streets between Odéon and the Seine. Travellers from all over the world come to this neighborhood for its fashionable boutiques, art galleries, and antique stores.

Also close to the Odéon station is St-Germain-des-Prés, one of the oldest churches in Paris. Construction on the first cathedral at this site began in the sixth century, but the most ancient parts of the existing church date back to the late tenth century. In the 1700s, the entire St-Germain quarter was home to the fashionable aristocracy of Paris. Although many of the noble mansions from that époque have been destroyed, the elegance and style associated with the neighborhood remain. Nearby cafés, including Brasserie Lipp, Les Deux Magots, and Café de Flore, were popular with such Paris luminaries as Picasso, de Beauvoir, Sartre, and Hemingway.

CHEZ ALLARD

CHEZ ALLARD

Coq au Vin
Chicken in Red Wine

Cassoulet Façon Allard
Cassoulet Allard Style

Canard aux Navets
Duck with New Turnips

Charlotte au Chocolat
Chocolate Charlotte

Coq au Vin

Chicken in Red Wine

This dish is a specialty of the house at Allard. Great for a party, it may be prepared a day or two before serving. In fact, coq au vin tastes even better when done ahead, because the flavors have a chance to blend. Accompany with steamed potatoes, rice, or noodles; a green salad; French bread; and the same red wine you used for cooking the chicken.

One 5-pound (2.5 kg) chicken, cut into serving pieces, or 5 pounds (2.5 kg) chicken pieces

Salt and freshly ground black pepper to taste

2 tablespoons rendered chicken fat, or 1 tablespoon butter and 1 tablespoon olive oil

7 ounces (220 g) bacon, cut crosswise into ¼-inch (6-mm) pieces

3 onions, chopped

3 garlic cloves, crushed

1 pound (500 g) mushrooms, quartered

1 tablespoon tomato paste

1 cup (8 fl oz/250 ml) Cognac or brandy

8 cups (2 l) dry red wine, such as Burgundy, Oregon Pinot Noir, or Zinfandel

Bouquet garni: 1 parsley sprig, 1 thyme sprig, and 1 bay leaf, tied in a cheesecloth square

2 tablespoons butter at room temperature

3 tablespoons flour

Generously sprinkle the chicken pieces with salt and pepper. In a large sauté pan or skillet over medium heat, melt the chicken fat, or melt the butter with the oil, and brown the chicken pieces, in batches if necessary, well all over, 12 to 16 minutes. Transfer the chicken to a large, heavy casserole with a lid or a Dutch oven.

In the same sauté pan or skillet, fry the bacon over medium heat until the fat is rendered and the bacon is golden brown, about 5 minutes.

Sprinkle the bacon pieces over the chicken. Sauté the onions and garlic in the bacon fat for 5 minutes, or until golden. Using a slotted spoon, transfer the onion mixture to the chicken. Add the mushrooms to the same pan, season with salt, and sauté for 5 minutes, or until the mushroom liquid evaporates. Using a slotted spoon, transfer the mushrooms to a plate and set aside.

Stir the tomato paste and Cognac or brandy into the pan with the chicken, heat, and carefully ignite with a long-handled match. When the flames subside, pour in the red wine. Add the bouquet garni and salt and pepper to taste. Cover and cook over low heat for 45 minutes, or until the chicken is tender when pierced with a fork.

Using a slotted spoon, transfer the chicken to a large plate; cover with aluminum foil to keep warm.

Bring the sauce to a boil over high heat and cook to reduce by half. In a small bowl, mash the butter with the flour to make a paste and whisk it into the sauce until smooth and thickened. Season with salt and pepper to taste. Add the chicken and the mushrooms and simmer for 5 minutes to heat through. Serve now, or cover and refrigerate for 1 to 2 days. Reheat, covered, in a low oven.

Makes 6 servings

Cassoulet Façon Allard

Cassoulet Allard Style

This hearty dish of beans baked with a variety of meats is perfect for a week-end lunch or a dinner party on a winter evening. Begin your preparations a day or two before you plan to serve the dish. The assembled cassoulet may be refrigerated and baked a day or two later. Serve piping hot directly from the pot or casserole in which the cassoulet was cooked, accompanied with a green salad, a Beaujolais or strong dry white wine, and fruit for dessert.

4½ cups (2 lb/1 kg) dried white beans (Great Northern or navy)

1 onion, quartered, plus 3 onions, chopped

4 bouquets garnis (in each: 2 parsley sprigs, 1 thyme sprig, 2 peppercorns, and 1 bay leaf, tied in a cheesecloth square)

Salt and freshly ground black pepper to taste

6 tablespoons (3 oz/90 g) rendered goose or duck fat (see Resources), or 3 tablespoons butter and 3 tablespoons oil

1 pound (500 g) lamb stew meat (boned lamb shoulder), trimmed of fat and cut into 1-inch (2.5 cm) cubes

3 tomatoes, quartered

3 teaspoons tomato paste

3 garlic cloves, crushed

6 tablespoons (2 oz/60 g) flour

6 cups (1.5 l) dry white wine

12 cups (3 l) veal stock (see Basics) or canned beef broth

1 pound (500 g) boned pork shoulder, trimmed of fat and cut into 1-inch (2.5-cm) cubes

1 pound (500 g) goose or duck confit (see Resources), fat scraped off and goose or duck cut into serving pieces, or smoked or roasted goose or duck, cut into 1-inch (2.5 cm) cubes

3 pork sausages, browned and sliced

Pick over and rinse the beans. Place them in a bowl, cover with cold water, and soak overnight; drain and set aside.

In a soup pot or stockpot, combine the beans, the quartered onion, 1 of the bouquets garnis, and cold water to cover by 3 inches (7.5 cm). Bring to a boil, reduce heat to low, cover, and simmer, stirring occasionally, until the beans are tender, about 1 hour and 45 minutes. Season with salt and pepper after 1½ hours.

In a large flameproof casserole or Dutch oven over medium heat, melt 2 tablespoons of the goose or duck fat or melt the butter with the oil and brown the lamb on all sides; season with salt and pepper to taste. Using a slotted spoon, transfer the lamb to a large plate. Sauté one third of the chopped onion in the same pan for 5 minutes, or until golden. Using a slotted spoon, transfer the onion to a bowl.

Return the lamb to the pan. Spoon the onion over the lamb and add 1 of the quartered tomatoes, 1 teaspoon of the tomato paste, 1 garlic clove, 1 of the bouquets garnis, and salt and pepper to taste. Sprinkle over 2 tablespoons of the flour and stir well. Add 2 cups (16 fl oz/500 ml) of the wine and 4 cups (1 l) of the stock or broth. Cover and simmer over medium-low heat for 1½ hours, or until the meat is very tender.

Repeat this process with the pork and then the goose or duck, with the same ingredients in the same proportions, cooking each meat separately. Using a slotted spoon, transfer the meats to a large casserole or Dutch oven. Arrange the sausage slices on top. Drain the beans and transfer them to a large bowl. Add all the meat pan juices to the beans and stir to mix. Pour the bean mixture over the meats. The casserole may be refrigerated at this point until ready for final cooking.

Preheat the oven to 475°F (245°C). If the casserole has been refrigerated, bring it to a simmer on top of the stove. Bake, uncovered, in the preheated oven for 20 to 30 minutes, or until a crust has formed. Serve the cassoulet hot from the oven.

Makes 12 servings

Canard aux Navets

Duck with New Turnips

This classic recipe by Marthe Allard, the bistro's first cook, is best made with baby turnips, as the flavor of mature turnips is too strong. The duck is served medium rare, in the French style.

1 duck, 4 to 5 pounds (2 to 2.5 kg)

6 tablespoons (3 oz/90 g) butter at room temperature

Salt to taste

⅓ cup (3 fl oz/80 ml) veal stock (see Basics) or water

3 tablespoons rendered duck or chicken fat (see Resources),
  or 1½ tablespoons butter and 1½ tablespoons olive oil

3 pounds (1.5 kg) baby turnips, peeled and halved

1 tablespoon sugar

Preheat the oven to 450°F (230°C). Remove the giblets and all visible fat from the duck. Smear 2 tablespoons of the butter over the breast, sprinkle with salt, and prick the skin with a fork along the thighs, back, and lower part of the breast. Bake in the preheated oven for 15 minutes. Reduce the oven temperature to 350°F (180°C) and bake for 30 to 40 minutes, or until the juices run pale rose when a thigh is pricked with a fork.

Pour off the fat in the baking pan and stir in the remaining 4 tablespoons (2 oz/60 g) butter over medium heat until melted. Pour in the stock or water, stir to scrape up the browned bits from the bottom of the pan, and boil for 5 minutes.

In a medium sauté pan or skillet over medium heat, melt the chicken fat or melt the butter with the oil and sauté the turnips until golden on all sides. Sprinkle with the sugar and salt to taste and sauté for 5 minutes, or until the sugar has caramelized to a light brown. Pour in some of the cooking juices from the duck and simmer for 3 minutes, or until the turnips are tender.

To serve, thinly slice the duck and arrange the slices on a warmed serving platter with the turnips in the center. Spoon on the sauce and serve immediately.

Makes 4 servings

Charlotte au Chocolat

Chocolate Charlotte

At Allard, this rich chocolate dessert is traditionally served with crème anglaise. The mousse may be made several days in advance and refrigerated.

4 ounces (125 g) semisweet chocolate, chopped

2 tablespoons plus ⅓ cup (3 fl oz/80 ml) water

1¼ cups (10 oz/315 g) superfine sugar

3 eggs, separated

⅞ cup (7 oz/220 g) cold butter, cut into small pieces

⅓ cup (3 fl oz/80 ml) rum

20 to 30 ladyfingers (see Basics) or 3-by-1-by-½-inch
  (7.5 cm-by-2.5 cm-12-mm) strips sponge cake

2 cups (16 fl oz/500 g) crème anglaise (see Basics) for serving

Line the bottom of a 4-cup (1 l) mold or a bowl with plastic wrap.

In a double boiler over simmering water, combine the chocolate, the 2 tablespoons water, and ¼ cup (125 g) of the sugar and stir until the chocolate melts.

Whisk in the egg yolks until smooth and creamy; do not boil. Remove from heat and whisk in the butter one piece at a time, until well blended.

In a large bowl, beat the egg whites until stiff, glossy peaks form. Stir one fourth of the whites into the chocolate mixture. Gently fold the remaining whites into the chocolate mixture until thoroughly blended.

Meanwhile, in a small saucepan, combine the remaining 1 cup (220 g) sugar, the ⅓ cup (3 fl oz) water, and the rum. Cook over medium-high heat until the sugar dissolves and the liquid is syrupy.

One by one, dip the ladyfingers or sponge cake strips into the syrup for a second. Arrange them inside the mold or bowl, pressing them closely together, with the curved sides of the ladyfingers against the bottom and sides of the mold or bowl. Reserve the remaining ladyfingers or strips.

Pour the chocolate mixture into the mold, covering the ladyfingers or strips. Smooth the surface and use the reserved ladyfingers or strips to cover the top of the mousse. Cover with plastic wrap and set a saucer or small plate on top. Top with a weight such as a soup can and refrigerate for at least 12 hours or up to 3 days before serving.

To serve, remove the weight and plastic wrap from the top and run a knife around the inside edge of the mold or bowl. Place a chilled serving dish upside down over the charlotte and reverse the two so the charlotte drops onto the dish. Peel off the remaining wrap. Slice the charlotte and serve with the crème anglaise. Refrigerate if not serving immediately.

Makes 8 servings

ASTIER

44, RUE JEAN-PIERRE-TIMBAUD, 75011 PARIS

MÉTRO PARMENTIER

Astier is a true neighborhood bistro. The decor is simple—elbow-to-elbow tables, warm lighting, and a small wooden bar—and Chef Clerc's menu is magnificent. Waiters and waitresses, including Monsieur Vergnaud, Astier's young owner, go flying up and down the steep and extremely narrow staircase between the two dining areas, while patrons line up outside. However without a reservation, chances for a table here are slim. Astier fills quickly with a mixed crowd of devoted habitués—Parisians who know where to go for generous portions of first-class bistro cuisine.

According to legend, the original building on this corner housed a cabaret and meeting place for the local underworld. In fact, during a recent renovation of the bistro's wine cellar, piles of antique weapons were found buried in the building's foundation! By the 1900s, Le Moulin Rouge, as the restaurant was then called, had closed its doors. Then in 1956, Monsieur Astier, an Auvergne native, opened his bistro in the eleventh arrondissement. The current owner and chef have been at Astier for over a decade.

Chef Clerc's superb bistro classics are not to be missed, and Astier's cheese course, which in typical French fashion follows the main course, is especially memorable. An immense low-rimmed basket passed from table to table includes a vast selection of cheeses, including three or four different *chèvres* (goat cheeses), Bries, Camemberts, and many regional cheeses, all at the perfect stage of ripeness.

NEIGHBORHOOD WALK

Astier is in the eleventh arrondissement, traditionally a working-class enclave and home to immigrants from abroad as well as French people from the provinces. Energy and money were brought into the neighborhood in the late 1980s, when the new Paris opera house was constructed on the former site of the Bastille, the infamous prison that was demolished at the start of the French Revolution. The area is a popular destination for fashionable Parisians, and the streets around the opera house are crowded with restaurants, galleries, and boutiques. The Bastille area is only a short métro ride from Astier, but if you're in the mood to walk, the warehouses, workshops, and residential neighborhoods of the eleventh arrondissement are an interesting change from the usual tourist destinations in Paris.

Another easy walk or métro ride from Astier, along rue de la République, is the most famous cemetery in Paris, Père Lachaise. Entering this walled cemetery is like walking into a strange village. Many tombs and mausoleums are built to resemble miniature houses or castles, and the alleys between them have names, as if they were streets. The monuments at Père Lachaise stretch on and on, sometimes crumbling and cracked like ancient ruins, sometimes as pristine and carefully designed as modern art. It's a good idea to stop at the entrance for a map, particularly if there are certain graves you want to visit. Chopin, Bizet, Gertrude Stein, Jim Morrison, and Edith Piaf are among the many famous figures buried here.

ASTIER

Les Oeufs Cocotte en Croûte

Baked Eggs in Ramekins with Pastry Crust

Lapin à la Moutarde

Rabbit with Mustard Sauce

La Terrine d'Agrumes
et Son Coulis d'Oranges

Citrus Terrine with Orange Coulis

Oeufs en Cocotte en Croûte

Baked Eggs in Ramekins with Pastry Crust

This dish is a specialty of the house at Astier. If you do not have foie gras, chopped morels are a good substitute; if you use morels, leave out the truffle. Thawed frozen puff pastry may be used in place of homemade puff pastry.

Four 5½-inch-diameter (14-cm) puff pastry rounds (see Basics)

1½ ounces (45 g) chilled foie gras (see Resources), sliced,
  or morels, finely chopped, and 2 tablespoons unsalted butter

1 teaspoon clarified butter (see Basics)

4 teaspoons demi-glace (see Resources) or reduced beef stock
  or broth (see Basics)

8 tablespoons (4 fl oz/125 ml) heavy cream

8 eggs

Salt and freshly ground black pepper to taste

½ teaspoon Cognac or brandy

½ teaspoon port

⅙ ounce (5 g) black truffle, sliced (optional)

Preheat the oven to 400°F (200°C). Arrange the pastry rounds on a baking sheet and bake in the preheated oven for 30 minutes, or until golden brown; set aside.

Reduce the oven temperature to 350°F (180°C). Butter eight 5-inch-diameter (13-cm) ramekins or custard cups.

Using a sharp knife that has been dipped into boiling water for each slice, cut the foie gras, if using, into eight ¼-inch-thick (6-mm) round slices. Cover the slices and chill for at least 20 minutes, or until cooking time. Film the bottom of a medium sauté pan or skillet with the clarified butter and heat over high heat until very hot but not burning. Sauté the foie gras slices for less than 1 minute on each side, or until just browned around the edges. Transfer the foie gras to a plate. If using the morels, melt the 2 tablespoons butter in a sauté pan over medium-high heat and sauté the mushrooms for 5 minutes, or until the liquid evaporates. Transfer the mushrooms to a plate.

Place the ramekins or cups in a baking dish and fill the baking dish with boiling water to reach halfway up the sides of the ramekins or cups.

Place 1 teaspoon of the demi-glace or reduced stock or broth and 1 tablespoon of the cream into each ramekin; stir to blend. Break 2 eggs into each ramekin or cup and sprinkle with salt and pepper. In a small bowl, mix the remaining 4 tablespoons (2 fl oz/60 ml) cream, the port, and Cognac or brandy. Pour one fourth of this mixture into each ramekin or cup. Add a foie gras slice and a truffle slice, if using. Bake in the preheated oven for 20 minutes. Remove from the oven. Place a puff pastry circle on top of each ramekin and heat in the oven for 3 minutes. Serve immediately.

Makes 4 servings

Lapin à la Moutarde

Rabbit with Mustard Sauce

Rabbit with mustard sauce is a bistro favorite. This recipe also works well with chicken. Ask the butcher to cut the rabbit into hind-leg and foreleg pieces and to bone the loin portions. The dish can be prepared 1 day ahead and rewarmed over low heat just before serving. Serve with fresh tagliatelle or other noodles and accompany with a Pinot Noir, Merlot or Sauvignon Blanc.

2 tablespoons olive oil

One rabbit, 2 to 3 pounds (1 to 1.5 kg), cut into 4 serving pieces

Salt and freshly ground black pepper to taste

3 tablespoons unsalted butter

1 onion, diced

2 cups (16 fl oz/500 ml) dry white wine

1 tablespoon Dijon mustard

About 4 cups (1 l) chicken stock (see Basics) or canned low-salt
   chicken broth, or as needed to just cover the meat

Mustard Cream Sauce

1½ cups (12 fl oz/375 ml) heavy cream

⅓ cup (3 oz/90 g) Dijon mustard

Pinch of chopped fresh tarragon

In a large, flameproof casserole or Dutch oven over medium-high heat, heat the olive oil until fragrant. Brown the rabbit pieces for about 2 minutes on each side; season with salt and pepper. Transfer the rabbit to a plate and set aside. Discard the oil.

In the same pan, melt the butter over medium heat and sauté the onion for 5 minutes, or until soft. Add the wine, mustard, salt, and pepper. Stir to scrape up any browned bits from the bottom of the pan. Return the rabbit pieces to the pan, pour in enough stock or broth to just cover, and bring to a boil. Reduce heat to medium and simmer, uncovered, for 45 minutes, or until the meat is tender when pierced with a fork and falls easily away from the bone.

To make the sauce: In a small saucepan, bring all the ingredients to a boil and cook for about 20 minutes, or until reduced by one third.

Serve the rabbit from its casserole, with the sauce alongside, or on a platter with the sauce poured over it.

Makes 4 servings

Opposite: La Terrine d'Agrumes (page 52)

La Terrine d'Agrumes et son Coulis d'Orange

Citrus Terrine with Orange Coulis

A slice of this pretty, flavorful dessert makes a light and refreshing finish to a meal.

½ cup (4 fl oz/125 ml) water

1 envelope plain gelatin

2 small pink grapefruits, peeled and sectioned (see Basics)

4 oranges, peeled and sectioned (see Basics)

½ cup (4 fl oz/125 ml)) simple syrup (see Basics)

¼ cup (2 fl oz/60 ml) Grand Marnier

Orange Coulis

1 orange, zested (see Basics) peeled, quartered, and seeded

1 cup (8 fl oz/250 ml) simple syrup (see Basics)

32 fresh raspberries, or ⅓ cup (3 fl oz/80 ml) crème de cassis, for garnish

Pour ¼ cup (2 fl oz/60 ml) of the water into a saucepan and sprinkle in the gelatin; let soak for 1 minute. Add the remaining ¼ cup (2 fl oz/ 60 ml) water and stir over low heat for 5 minutes, or until the gelatin is completely dissolved.

In a medium bowl, gently combine the sectioned fruit, simple syrup, Grand Marnier, and gelatin mixture. Pour into a 9-by-5-inch (23-by-13-cm) terrine or loaf pan and press down the fruit until it is compact and completely covered with the liquid. Cover with plastic wrap and refrigerate for at least 4 hours or up to 48 hours before serving.

To make the coulis: In a food processor, purée the orange zest, orange flesh, and simple syrup.

To serve, spoon the coulis on each of 8 plates, top with a slice of the terrine, and garnish the coulis with 4 of the raspberries or dot it with cassis.

Makes one 9-by-5-inch terrine; serves 8

AUBERGE PYRÉNÉES-CÉVENNES

106, RUE DE LA FOLIE-MÉRICOURT, 75011 PARIS
MÉTRO RÉPUBLIQUE

Daniel and Françoise Constantin are following a long-standing tradition of husband-and-wife bistro owners. Daniel runs the kitchen at the Auberge Pyrénées-Cévennes, while Françoise, a native of Lyon, presides in the dining room. Thanks to the talented young couple, this bistro in the northwest corner of the eleventh arrondissement continues to be a noteworthy destination for Parisians and food-lovers from all over the world.

The Constantins bought the Auberge in 1998 from previous chef/owner Philippe Serbource. Included in the sale were the contents of the bistro's wine cellar. The cellar is at least three hundred years old, and a few of the precious bottles stored there (and available for consumption at the bistro) date back to the 1890s. Daniel Constantin has added some of his wife's favorite Lyonnais dishes to the bistro's menu, while continuing to serve his predecessors' Basque specialties. Both regions offer a hearty, rich cuisine—in fact, Robert de Niro dined regularly at L'Auberge Pyrénées-Cévennes when he needed to gain weight for his role as Jake La Motta in the movie *Raging Bull!*

Auberge means inn or tavern in French, and the exposed beam ceiling, hanging hams and sausages, friendly blue and white checkered tablecloths, and copper pots on the walls provide just the right cozy, country-style ambience.

NEIGHBORHOOD WALK

One of the most beautiful squares in Paris, the place des Vosges, is a brief walk or subway ride from the Auberge Pyrénées-Cévennes. Built in the early 1600s for Henri IV, the square was originally called the place Royal and acquired its present name when the Vosges region in eastern France was the first to pay taxes after the Revolution. In the late afternoon, a golden glow highlights the place des Vosges's matched brick mansions and the park becomes animated with Parisians on their way home from work, visitors resting on wooden benches, and young children playing among the trees. There's something about being surrounded by so much symmetry—and beauty—that creates a peaceful feeling rare in a modern-day city.

In the 1600s, the Marais (the area around the place des Vosges) was the center of fashionable Paris. Although most members of the aristocracy moved to the Left Bank neighborhood Faubourg St-Germain before the eighteenth century, the streets and buildings of the Marais have changed remarkably little during the last three hundred years. These days, the area is trendy once again, and its pre-revolutionary mansions are interspersed with galleries and stylish fashion boutiques. Just north of the place des Vosges is the Musée Picasso, a seventeenth-century mansion now devoted to the works of Pablo Picasso.

Auberge Pyrénées-Cévennes

Salade Lyonnaise

Frisée Salad with Bacon and Poached Egg

Petit Salé Lentilles

Lentils with Ham

Poires au Vin Beaujolais

Pears in Red Wine

Salade Lyonnaise

Frisée Salad with Bacon and Poached Egg

An old favorite to make a meal of at lunchtime or to serve as a first course for dinner. Serve with plenty of crusty French bread.

3 or 4 slices thick-cut bacon, or 4 ounces (125 g) slab bacon or Canadian bacon, rind removed

1 cup (2 oz/60 g) ½-inch-diced (12-mm) stale bread

Vinaigrette

2 tablespoons red wine vinegar

½ teaspoon Dijon mustard

Salt to taste

½ cup (4 fl oz/125 ml) soybean, peanut oil, or canola oil

2 small heads frisée (curly endive) torn into bite-sized pieces

1 tablespoon cider vinegar

4 eggs

Minced fresh parsley for garnish

Cut the bacon into ¼-inch (6-mm) slices or 1-inch (2.5 cm) cubes. In a skillet over medium heat, fry the bacon for 4 to 5 minutes, or until it begins to give off some fat. Add the diced bread and cook, stirring occasionally, until the croutons and bacon are evenly browned and crisp.

To make the vinaigrette: Whisk the vinegar, mustard, and salt together. Gradually whisk in the oil in a very thin stream to make a thick dressing.

Toss the frisée with the vinaigrette and half the bacon and croutons. Sprinkle the rest of the bacon and croutons on top.

In a large sauté pan or skillet, bring 2 inches (5 cm) water to a simmer. Stir in the vinegar. One at a time, break each egg into a saucer and slip it into the simmering water. Poach the eggs for 4 minutes. Divide the salad among 4 plates. Using a slotted spoon, remove each egg from the water and place it on top of a salad. Garnish the whites of each egg with parsley and serve immediately.

Makes 4 servings

AUBERGE PYRÉNÉES-CÉVENNES

Petit Salé Lentilles

Lentils with Ham

A plate of lentils and ham is an old-fashioned bistro specialty. Serve with a robust Gamay or Côtes-du-Rhone.

2 pounds (1 kg) meaty ham hocks or shanks

2¼ cups (1 lb/500 g) French green lentils (*lentilles de Puy*)

1 onion, sliced

2 carrots, peeled and sliced

1 fresh thyme sprig

1 bay leaf

Salt and freshly ground black pepper to taste

Bring a large pot of water to a boil and add the ham. Reduce heat to low and simmer, partially covered, for 45 minutes. Drain and remove the meat from the hocks.

Pick over and rinse the lentils. Put the lentils in a large saucepan and add the onion, carrots, thyme, bay leaf, and water to cover by 3 inches (7.5 cm). Bring to a boil, reduce heat to low, and simmer gently for about 35 minutes, or until tender but firm. Season with salt and pepper.

To serve, ladle the lentils onto 4 dinner plates. Arrange some of the ham on top and serve immediately.

Makes 4 servings

Poires au Vin Beaujolais

Pears in Red Wine

Prepare this simple, non-fat dessert one day before serving. It makes a refreshing finish to a heavy meal.

½ bottle (375 ml) fruity red wine such as a Beaujolais

½ cup (4 oz/125 g) sugar

1 cup (8 fl oz/250 ml) water

6 firm pears

In a large, nonreactive saucepan, bring the wine and sugar to a boil. Add the water and simmer for 5 minutes.

While the liquid is simmering, peel, core, and quarter the pears. Place the pears in a serving bowl and pour the hot wine mixture over. Cover with plastic wrap and refrigerate for 24 hours before serving.

Makes 6 servings

BALTHAZAR

——◆◇◆——

80 SPRING STREET, NEW YORK, NY 10012

Celebrated restaurateur Keith McNally opened Balthazar in 1997, and it's been almost impossible to find a vacant seat ever since. Both cuisine and decor at this New York bistro live up to the standard of the best of its Parisian counterparts. A handsome mosaic tile floor, antique mirrors, small paper-covered tables, red leather banquettes, and nostalgic music create an authentic, old-fashioned bistro atmosphere, especially when combined with crowds of happy, satisfied diners.

Co-chefs Less Hanson and Riad Nasr met when they were both working at New York's four-star Restaurant Daniel. The two young men, both with impeccable resumés, were delighted when McNally approached them about his new bistro. Their collaboration seems to be working—Balthazar's cuisine has won rave reviews, and dishes like Steak Frites (page 75), Warm Goat Cheese Tart (page 63), and the fabulous *plateau de fruits de mer* (fresh seafood platter) provide those of us on this side of the Atlantic with a chance to experience true bistro cuisine at surprisingly reasonable prices. Balthazar's impressive all-French wine list includes more than 175 labels, and the adjoining Balthazar bakery supplies New Yorkers with delicious take-out soups, salads, sandwiches, breads, and pastries.

BALTHAZAR

Warm Goat Cheese Tart
with Caramelized Onions

Roast Beet and Mâche Salad
with Haricots Verts, Leeks,
and Walnut Vinaigrette

Braised Short Ribs

Pots de Crème au Chocolat

Chocolate Custards

Warm Goat Cheese Tart
with Caramelized Onions

Serve a slice of this delicious tart as an appetizer, or a larger slice along with a salad as a main course.

Pastry

1¾ cups (9 oz/280 g) all-purpose flour

Pinch of salt

½ cup (4 oz/125 g) unsalted butter, cut into cubes

2 egg yolks, beaten

3 to 4 teaspoons cold water

Filling

1 tablespoon olive oil

1 large onion, sliced

Leaves from 1 fresh thyme sprig, minced

1 bay leaf

Salt and freshly ground black pepper to taste

8 ounces (250 g) goat cheese at room temperature

8 ounces (250 g) cream cheese at room temperature

2 eggs

⅔ cup (5 fl oz/160 ml) heavy cream

To make the pastry: In a medium bowl, stir the flour and salt together. Cut in the butter with a pastry cutter or 2 knives until the mixture is the texture of coarse crumbs. Add the egg yolks and water and mix quickly with a fork. Press the dough together with your fingers. Alternatively, add all the ingredients to a food processor and process just until the dough just comes together. Pat the dough into a flat disk, cover with plastic wrap, and refrigerate for at least 30 minutes.

Preheat the oven to 350°F (180°C). On a flat surface, roll the pastry dough out to a 12-inch (30-cm) circle. Fit the pastry into a 10-inch (25 cm) tart pan with a removable bottom. Line with aluminum foil and fill with dried beans or pie weights. Place on a baking sheet and bake in the preheated oven for 9 or 10 minutes, or until set. Remove from the oven and remove the foil and beans or weights. Prick the bottom of the shell with a fork. Return the shell to the oven and bake for 3 or 4 minutes, or until lightly browned. Remove from the oven and let cool in the pan on a wire rack.

Preheat the oven to 350°F (180°C). To make the filling: In a small sauté pan or skillet over medium heat, heat the olive oil and sauté the onion, thyme, and bay leaf for about 7 minutes, or until the onion is golden. Remove and discard the bay leaf. Season the onion mixture with salt and pepper and set aside.

In a blender or food processor, combine the goat cheese, cream cheese, eggs, cream, and salt and pepper to taste. Process until perfectly smooth.

Spread the onion mixture evenly over the bottom of the tart shell and fill with the cheese mixture. Bake in the preheated oven for 12 minutes, or until a knife inserted in the center comes out clean. Let cool slightly or to room temperature. Cut the tart into wedges and serve.

Makes 8 servings

Roast Beet and Mâche Salad with Haricots Verts, Leeks, and Walnut Vinaigrette

Roasting root vegetables concentrates and rounds out their flavor. Beets especially benefit from this treatment, whether they are served hot or cold. This salad balances the contrasting flavors of sweet beets, nutty green beans, and tart goat cheese.

4 beets

2 tablespoons vegetable oil

4 fresh thyme sprigs

4 ounces (125 g) haricots verts or baby Blue Lake green beans, chopped into 2-inch (5-cm) pieces

Vinaigrette

¼ cup (2 fl oz/60 ml) sherry wine vinegar

1 teaspoon Dijon mustard

¾ cup (6 fl oz/180 ml) grapeseed or canola oil

¼ cup (2 fl oz/60 ml) cold-pressed walnut oil

Salt and freshly ground black pepper to taste

4 leeks, white part only

4 ounces (125 g) mâche (lamb's lettuce) or frisée (curly endive)

2 tablespoons walnuts, chopped and toasted (see Basics)

4 ounces (125 g) goat cheese, cut into slivers

Preheat the oven to 375°F (190°C). In a large bowl, toss the beets with the oil. Separately wrap each beet and a sprig of thyme in a square of aluminum foil. Roast in the preheated oven for 1 hour, or until the beets are tender when pierced with a knife. Unwrap and let cool.

In a large pot of salted boiling water, cook the green beans for 5 to 10 minutes, or until crisp-tender. Using a slotted spoon or a wire-mesh skimmer, transfer the beans to a bowl of cold water. Drain and set aside. In the boiling bean water, cook the leeks for 10 to 15 minutes, or until tender. Drain and let cool.

To make the vinaigrette: In a medium bowl, whisk the vinegar and mustard together. Gradually whisk in the oils until emulsified. Season with salt and pepper.

Peel the beets. Using a sharp knife or mandoline, thinly slice the beets and arrange the slices to cover 4 salad plates. Brush the beets with vinaigrette. In 2 medium bowls, toss the green beans and leeks separately with the remaining vinaigrette. Arrange the green beans on top of the beets and top them with a mound of leeks. Add a bouquet of lettuce in the center. Sprinkle with toasted walnuts and garnish with slivers of goat cheese. Serve immediately.

Makes 8 servings

Braised Short Ribs

Braised short ribs are the plat du jour every Saturday night at Balthazar. This dish is so delicious and simple to prepare that you'll enjoy making it at home. Serve with mashed potatoes and mixed root vegetables.

2 tablespoons vegetable oil

6 to 8 pounds (3 to 4 kg) thick and meaty short ribs

2 carrots, peeled and chopped

2 celery stalks, chopped

2 onions, chopped

6 to 8 shallots, chopped

1 tablespoon tomato paste

¼ cup all-purpose flour

1 head garlic, halved crosswise

Bouquet garni: 1 parsley sprig, 1 thyme sprig, 1 bay leaf, 3 peppercorns, and 2 cloves, tied in a cheesecloth square

1 bottle (750 ml) full-bodied red wine

½ cup (4 fl oz/125 ml) ruby port

4 cups (1 l) veal stock (see Basics) or canned low-salt beef broth

Salt and freshly ground black pepper to taste

Preheat the oven to 350°F (180°C). In a large, flameproof casserole or Dutch oven over medium-high heat, heat the oil and brown the meat on all sides. Using a slotted spoon, transfer the meat to a plate and set aside.

In the same pan, sauté the carrots, celery, onions, and shallots for 5 to 10 minutes, or until lightly browned. Stir in the tomato paste. Sprinkle with flour and cook 3 to 4 minutes longer, stirring to scrape up the browned bits from the bottom of the pan. Add the meat, garlic, bouquet garni, wine, and port. Increase heat to high and cook to reduce the liquid by half. Pour in the stock or broth and bring to a boil. Cover and bake in the preheated oven for 3 hours, or until the meat is fork tender.

Using a slotted spoon, transfer the meat to a serving dish and cover with aluminum foil to keep warm. Strain the sauce through a fine-meshed sieve and return it to the pan. Cook over high heat to reduce the sauce to a nice gravylike consistency. Season with salt and pepper. Pour the sauce over the short ribs and serve.

Makes 8 servings

Pots de Crème au Chocolat

Chocolate Custards

A rich, silky pudding that melts on the tongue and has a deep chocolate flavor. Use the best-quality chocolate you can find. Serve with strong coffee, a vintage port, or perhaps a Banyuls wine.

4 teaspoons sugar

1½ cups (12 fl oz/375 ml) heavy cream

1 cup (8 fl oz/250 ml) whole milk

8 ounces (250 g) bittersweet chocolate, chopped

12 egg yolks

Unsweetened cocoa powder and powdered sugar for dusting

Preheat the oven to 300°F (150°C). In a saucepan, combine the sugar, cream, and milk and bring just to a boil over medium heat. Stir in the chocolate and bring back to a boil, stirring often; remove from heat.

In a large bowl, whisk the egg yolks until pale. Gradually whisk in the hot cream mixture.

Arrange 8 individual ovenproof ramekins or custard cups in a baking pan and pour in the chocolate mixture. Add hot water to the baking pan reach halfway up the sides of the ramekins or cups. Bake in the preheated oven for 20 to 30 minutes, or until the custards are puffed and still tremble slightly. Remove from the oven and let cool completely. Refrigerate for at least 2 hours before serving. Serve cold, dusted with a little cocoa and powdered sugar.

Makes 8 custards

BOUCHON

6534 WASHINGTON STREET, YOUNTVILLE, CA 94599

Bouchon, a word used for bistros in the French city of Lyon, was established in 1998 by brothers Thomas and Joseph Keller. Instantaneously popular, the bistro is now a favorite haunt in the Napa Valley wine country.

Thomas Keller is chef/owner of the internationally acclaimed French Laundry in Yountville, and Joseph Keller is chef/owner of the historic Woodbox Inn on Nantucket Island. Together they have created a bistro with an authentic French menu, a wisely chosen list of wines from local vintners, and an informal, stylish atmosphere. The interior was designed by Adam D. Tihany, who is known for his work at Le Cirque 2000 in New York and at Spago in Las Vegas. The bistro's handcrafted zinc bar, etched glass panels, witty mural by artist Paulin Paris, burgundy velvet banquettes, and antique French sconces and sideboards create a sophisticated interpretation of a French bistro.

Chefs Jeffrey Cerciello and Joshua Schwartz, who both worked with Thomas Keller at The French Laundry, serve impeccably executed French bistro classics. House specialties include roasted chicken, Steak Frites (page 75), and a cold seafood platter for two that includes lobster, shrimp, oysters, clams, and black mussels. Pastry chef Shuna Lydon's dessert listings include a luscious tarte Tatin, profiteroles, and a refreshing Lemon Tart (page 79).

BOUCHON

Swiss Chard and Fingerling Potato Quiche

Steak Frites

Steak with French Fries

Cauliflower au Gratin

Lemon Tart

Swiss Chard and Fingerling Potato Quiche

If Comté cheese is unavailable, substitute Gruyère. Chef Joshua Schwartz suggests that you give each salad a squeeze of fresh lemon juice just before serving.

Pastry

½ cup (2½ oz/75 g) plus ⅓ cup (2 oz/60 g) all-purpose flour

⅓ cup (1 oz/30 g) cake flour

⅛ teaspoon baking powder

Pinch of salt

½ cup (4 oz/125 g) butter

¼ cup (2 fl oz/60 ml) water

Filling

2 tablespoons butter

2 shallots, minced

9 ounces (250 g) Swiss chard, chopped

Salt and ground white pepper to taste

3 eggs

1 cup (8 fl oz/250 ml) heavy cream

1 cup (8 fl oz/250 ml) milk

Ground nutmeg to taste

5 ounces (155 g) fingerling potatoes, sliced

⅓ cup (1½ oz/45 g) shredded Comté cheese

Salad

Leaves from 2 heads Bibb lettuce

2 shallots, minced

2 tablespoons minced fresh flat-leaf (Italian) parsley

2 tablespoons minced fresh chives

2 tablespoons minced fresh chervil

⅓ cup (3 fl oz/80 ml) to ½ cup (4 fl oz/125 ml) vinaigrette
(see Basics)

To make the pastry: In a medium bowl, stir together the all-purpose flour, cake flour, baking powder, and salt. Cut in the butter with a pastry cutter or 2 knives until the mixture resembles coarse crumbs. Stir in the water with a fork. Press the dough together with your fingers to make a ball. Alternatively, add the flour, butter, and salt to a blender or food processor and process until the mixture resembles coarse crumbs, about 15 seconds. With the motor running, pour in the water in a steady stream and process until the dough begins to form a ball, about 20 seconds. Flatten the dough into a disc, cover with plastic wrap, and refrigerate for at least 45 minutes.

Preheat the oven to 350°F (180°C). On a lightly floured surface, roll the dough out to an 11-inch (28-cm) circle. Fit the dough into a 10-inch (25-cm) quiche mold. Run a rolling pin over the top to trim the dough. Prick the bottom and sides of the pastry with a fork. Line the pastry with aluminum foil and fill with dried beans or pastry weights. Bake in the pre-heated oven for 20 minutes. Remove the foil and beans or weights; set aside and let cool.

In a large sauté pan or skillet over medium heat, melt the butter and sauté the shallots and Swiss chard for 3 minutes. Season with salt and pepper; set aside.

In a large bowl, whisk the eggs, milk, and cream together until well blended. Generously season with salt, white pepper, and nutmeg to taste. Stir in the drained chard mixture. Pour the filling into the partially baked pastry shell. Top with the sliced potatoes, then sprinkle with the cheese. Bake in the preheated oven for 30 to 40 minutes, or until set. Remove from the oven and let cool to room temperature.

In a large salad bowl, toss all the salad ingredients together. Serve each quiche slice with a small salad.

Makes 6 servings

Steak Frites

Steak with French Fries

This must be the quintessential bistro dish.

Maître d'Hôtel Butter

½ cup (4 oz/125 g) butter at room temperature

Salt and freshly ground black pepper to taste

½ tablespoon minced fresh parsley

½ tablespoon fresh lemon juice

French Fries

8 russet potatoes

Peanut oil for deep-frying

Four 8-ounce (250 g) top sirloin steaks

Salt and freshly ground black pepper to taste

¼ cup (2 oz/60 ml) canola oil

¼ cup (2 oz/60 g) butter

4 shallots, chopped

Leaves from ½ bunch fresh thyme, chopped

Salt and freshly ground pepper to taste

To make the butter: In a medium bowl, thoroughly blend all the ingredients together. Transfer to a piece of parchment or plastic wrap and roll to form a log. Refrigerate until ready to use.

To make the French fries: Peel the potatoes and cut into ¼-inch-thick (6-mm) slices. Cut each slice lengthwise into strips ¼ inch (6 mm) wide and 2½ inches (6 cm) long. Alternatively, use the French fry blade of a food processor. Fill a large bowl three-fourths full with water and add the potato strips.

Drain the potatoes and pat them very dry with paper towels. In a Dutch oven or deep fryer, pour peanut oil to a depth of 3 inches (7.5 cm).

Heat to 300°F (150°C) on a deep-fat frying thermometer, or until a crust of bread becomes golden within moments of being dropped into the oil. Working in batches, slip the potatoes into the oil and fry until they stiffen and barely start to color, 6 to 8 minutes. Using a slotted spatula, transfer the potatoes to paper towels to drain. Let cool for at least 15 minutes or up to several hours at room temperature.

A few minutes before serving, heat the oil to 350°F (180°C). Working in batches, slip the potatoes into the oil and fry, turning occasionally, until they are crisp and golden brown, about 5 minutes. Using a slotted spoon, transfer to a tray lined with paper towels. Keep warm in a low oven while you cook the remaining potatoes.

Preheat the oven to 425°F (220°C). Pat the steaks dry with paper towels. Rub salt and pepper to taste onto both sides of each steak. In a large, ovenproof sauté pan or skillet over high heat, heat the canola oil until almost smoking. Add the steaks and cook, turning once, until browned on both sides, about 2 minutes. Pour off any excess oil from the pan and reduce heat to medium. Add the butter, shallots, and thyme and sauté for 2 or 3 minutes. Place the pan in the preheated oven and bake the steaks for 4 minutes for medium rare; the steaks should be springy to the touch when squeezed from the sides.

Transfer the steaks to 4 warmed plates. Top each steak with a slice of the maître d'hôtel butter. Sprinkle the French fries with salt and pepper and place a mound of fries alongside each steak. Serve immediately.

Makes 4 servings

Opposite: Cauliflower au Gratin (page 78)

Cauliflower au Gratin

Cauliflower has never tasted so good.

½ lemon

1 large cauliflower

2 tablespoons butter

1 tablespoon minced shallot

1 tablespoon minced garlic

1 cup (8 fl oz/250 ml) vegetable stock (see Basics)
or canned low-salt vegetable broth

1 cup (8 fl oz/250 ml) heavy cream

1 to 2 tablespoons horseradish or to taste

Salt and freshly ground black pepper to taste

½ cup (2 oz/60 g) shredded Gruyère cheese

Preheat the oven to 425°F (220°C). Squeeze the lemon into a medium bowl of water. Cut the cauliflower into small florets. Chop and reserve the stems. Soak the florets in the lemon water for 2 minutes. Blanch the florets in salted boiling water for 5 minutes, or until crisp-tender; drain and set aside.

In a medium sauté pan or skillet, melt the butter over low heat and sauté the reserved cauliflower stems, shallot, and garlic until soft; do not brown. Pour in the stock or broth, raise heat to high, and cook until the liquid entirely evaporates. Transfer to a blender or food processor, add the cream, and purée. Stir in the horseradish, salt, and pepper.

Toss the cauliflower florets with the cream mixture in an ovenproof terrine or casserole. Top with the shredded cheese and bake in the preheated oven for 20 minutes, or until golden brown. Serve immediately.

Makes 4 servings

Lemon Tart

This easy-to-prepare tart makes a delectable finale.

Pastry

1⅔ cups (9 oz/280 g) all-purpose flour

⅔ cup (3 oz/90 g) powdered sugar, sifted

⅔ cup (5 oz/155 g) cold butter, diced

1 egg, beaten

Filling

5 large eggs

1 egg yolk

1 cup (8 oz/250 g) sugar

1 cup (8 fl oz/250 ml) fresh lemon juice

½ cup (4 oz/125 g) butter

To make the pastry: Preheat the oven to 350°F (180°C). In a medium bowl, stir the flour and sugar together. Cut the butter into the flour mixture with a pastry cutter or 2 knives until the mixture resembles coarse crumbs. Using a fork, stir in the egg and mix just until the dough comes together. Pat the dough into a flat disk, cover with plastic wrap, and refrigerate for at least 30 minutes before rolling out.

On a lightly floured surface, roll out the dough into an 10-inch (25-cm) circle. Fit the dough into a 9-inch (23-cm) tart pan with a removable bottom and trim off the excess dough. Line the pastry with aluminum foil and fill with dried beans or pastry weights. Place on a baking sheet and bake in the preheated oven for 15 to 20 minutes, or until lightly browned. Remove the foil and beans or weights. Bake in the oven for 4 minutes, or until evenly light brown; set aside and let cool.

Reduce the oven temperature to 275°F (135°C). In a large bowl, whisk the eggs, egg yolk, and sugar together until pale.

In a small saucepan over medium heat, bring the lemon juice to a simmer; remove from heat. In another small saucepan, melt the butter over medium heat. Gradually whisk the hot lemon juice and butter into the egg mixture until thoroughly blended. Strain through a fine-meshed sieve and pour into the prepared tart shell. Bake in the preheated oven for 20 minutes, or until a knife inserted in the center comes out clean. Remove from the oven and let cool on a rack to cool on a wire rack. Serve at room temperature.

Makes one 9-inch (23-cm) tart; serves 8

LA CAGOUILLE

10, PLACE BRANCUSI, 75014 PARIS
MÉTRO GAÎTÉ

The decor of La Cagouille, Paris's fine fish bistro, is clean and modern. The dining room's slate floors, marble-topped tables, contemporary light fixtures, and walls draped with fishermen's ropes create a stylish atmosphere for seafood-lovers.

Gérard Allemandou, the talented chef/owner of La Cagouille, includes many dishes on the menu that are favorites from childhood. He is from the Charentes, the fish- and Cognac-rich region of the Atlantic coast north of Bordeaux. Monsieur Allemandou sent me the following recipe for cod (see page 86). Translated directly from the French, it illustrates the depth of his feelings about cooking and my delight at receiving such a passionate recipe.

Cod is the Atlantic's prime fish, hero of all the sagas, and subject of the cold-water fishing culture's eternal myths—from St-Malo and Granville to the Faroe islands, and the coastline of Canada. Cod. . . savior of men, currency, common link, long before the European Union, from the Basque country's *bacalao au pil pil* to the *stockfisch* of Auvergne and the *brandades* of Nîmes and Venise. . .

Today, with survival no longer a question for our country, drying cod is of secondary importance and luck is really a matter of being able to savor fresh cod.

Peel the garlic and slowly cook it in milk over low heat. Strain and add the butter to the cream, without allowing the mixture to come to a boil. In a sauté pan, sear the cod steaks and bake until done. On a warm plate, arrange a trace of yellow sauce, the brilliant cod, a handful of sea salt, freshly ground pepper, and a few new potatoes with a little semi-salted butter. Absolute happiness.

Neighborhood Walk

La Cagouille is in the heart of the Montparnasse district, famous for the many intellectuals and artists who lived near boulevard Montparnasse in the early 1900s. Montparnasse cafés, such as La Coupole, Le Dôme, and La Rotunde, were frequented by the likes of Picasso, Cocteau, Stravinsky, and Satie. Still open today, these Art Deco-style restaurants have retained some of their early glamour.

The Cimetière du Montparnasse, one of Paris's several park-like graveyards, is also just blocks away from La Cagouille. Surrounded by high walls and planted with trees, grasses, and flowers, the cemetery is a very peaceful place for an afternoon stroll—a reminder of Paris history and a nice respite after bustling boulevard Montparnasse. Another interesting afternoon could be spent at the nearby Catacombs. These ancient quarries, which stretch out underneath place Denfert-Rochereau, are stacked with bones from old Paris cemeteries and were the headquarters of the French Resistance during World War II.

Since the 1970s, the Tour Montparnasse has become the center, both visually and commercially, of Montparnasse. The tower, which is almost seven hundred feet high, houses offices and stores and offers a spectacular view of Paris from the fifty-sixth floor.

LA CAGOUILLE

Moules de Bouchots "Brûle-Doigts"

"Burn Your Fingers" Mussels

Pavé de Cabillaud à la Crème d'Ail Doux

Cod Steaks in Creamy Garlic Sauce

Tarte aux Pommes

Apple Tart

Moules de Bouchots "Brûle-Doigts"

"Burn Your Fingers" Mussels

A quick, easy way to serve fresh mussels. Gérard Allemandou, Cagouille's chef/owner, has indelible childhood memories of eating mussels like this right from the stove, which explains his name for the dish. "Burn Your Fingers" Mussels is almost always on the menu at La Cagouille. Serve with a nicely chilled Chablis or Fumé Blanc.

1½ pounds (750 g) black mussels, scrubbed and debearded

Freshly ground black pepper to taste

Crusty whole-wheat country bread and butter for serving

Heat a large cast-iron skillet over high heat until a drop of water sizzles and evaporates immediately. Add the mussels and shake the pan. Continue shaking until all the mussels have opened. Discard any mussels that do not open. Sprinkle the mussels generously with pepper. Serve immediately with bread and butter; bring the pan to the table or spoon the mussels into serving dishes.

Makes 4 first-course servings or 2 main-course servings

Pavé de Cabillaud
à la Crème d'Ail Doux

Cod Steaks in Creamy Garlic Sauce

Serve this dish with steamed new potatoes. If fresh cod is unavailable, substitute halibut, grouper, or other firm-fleshed white fish.

½ cup milk

2 garlic cloves, minced

⅓ cup (3 oz/90 g) butter, cut into small pieces

2 tablespoons vegetable oil

2 fresh cod steaks or fillets

Coarse sea salt and freshly ground black pepper to taste

In a small saucepan, combine the milk and garlic and simmer until the milk is reduced by half and the garlic is very soft. Strain through a fine-meshed sieve, pushing the garlic through with the back of a spoon. Return the milk to the saucepan and whisk in the butter one piece at a time; do not let boil.

In a medium sauté pan or skillet over medium-high heat, heat the oil and sauté the fish on one side for about 3 minutes, or until golden brown. Turn the fish over and cook for 5 to 6 minutes, or until golden brown on the second side and springy to the touch.

To serve, spoon some of the garlic sauce onto each of 2 warmed plates, top with a cod steak or fillet, and sprinkle with salt and pepper. Arrange 3 steamed new potatoes topped with butter on each plate and serve immediately.

Makes 2 servings

Opposite: Tarte aux Pommes (page 88)

Tarte aux Pommes

Apple Tart

This small open-faced apple tart is especially buttery and luscious.

One 6-inch (15-cm) square puff pastry (see Basics) or thawed
  frozen puff pastry

2 Granny Smith or Golden Delicious apples, peeled, cored, and
  very thinly sliced

2 tablespoons (1 oz/30 g) sugar

1 tablespoon cold butter, thinly shaved

½ cup (4 fl oz/125 ml) chilled heavy cream, whipped with sugar
  and vanilla extract to taste

Preheat the oven to 400°F (200°C). On a lightly floured board, roll the
puff pastry out to ⅛-inch (3-mm) thickness. Cut out a 6-inch-diameter
(15-cm) circle. Place the circle on a baking sheet. Prick the pastry all over
with a fork, going down through the dough to the baking sheet. Refrigerate
for 30 minutes.

Attractively arrange the thin apple slices in a spiral over the pastry, as
closely together as possible. Sprinkle evenly with the sugar and butter
shavings. Bake in the preheated oven for 30 minutes, or until the pastry is
golden brown. Serve with a large dollop of the flavored whipped cream.

Makes one 6-inch tart; serves 2

CHEZ DIANE

—∞◦∞—

25, RUE SERVANDONI, 75006 PARIS

MÉTRO ST-SULPICE

C hez Diane is a small, fashionable bistro just a few blocks from Place St-Sulpice, where many French publishing houses are headquarted. Across the street is the apartment building where William Faulkner lived during his stay in Paris.

Monsieur Derrieux, who has run Chez Diane since 1995, is originally from the Southwest of France. He likes to compare his bistro to a hidden corner of the countryside in the middle of Paris, a place where his patrons can experience some of the peace and tranquility he remembers from his native region.

In the evenings, Monsieur Derrieux's wife Diane, for whom the bistro is named, helps out in the dining room. But at lunchtime, the dining room's dozen tables are staffed by Monsieur Derrieux alone. Even so, he has time to spend a few minutes graciously chatting with guests at every table.

The seasonal menu at Chez Diane emphasizes simple, carefully prepared dishes with a focus on top-quality ingredients. Monsieur Derrieux personally makes sure that everything from the lettuces to the crème fraîche at his bistro are the best available. The same care can be seen in Chez Diane's decor, where soft yellow walls, a vintage tile floor, and lovely silvered mirrors create an ambience of style and comfort.

NEIGHBORHOOD WALK

Across the street from Chez Diane is the *Jardin du Luxembourg*, an example of the art of the French garden at its best. Luxembourg—with its grass that is certainly not for walking upon, gravel lined allés (paths), and carefully pruned trees—is quite formal, as is typical of public spaces in Paris. Overlooking the garden is the *Palais du Luxembourg*, now home to the French Senate. Constructed in the early 1600s for Marie de Médicis, widow of Henri IV, both the palace and its park reflect their past as an aristocratic residence.

For present day Parisians, the gardens are a welcome oasis of green in the center of their city. Students meet between classes in the park, couples stroll under the trees, groups of men spend long hours playing *les boules* (a bowling game similar to bocci ball that is popular in southern France), and children munch on an afternoon pastry or *crêpe* as they walk home from school. Sometimes it seems as if all of Paris is sitting in the green metal chairs around the octagonal pond where generations of French children have come to sail toy boats.

Servandoni street, where creamy stone buildings and gray cobblestones create an elegant Parisian color scheme, connects the Luxembourg garden with *place St-Sulpice*. This square is dominated by the St-Sulpice cathedral, built in the seventeenth and eighteenth centuries and known for its Delacroix frescoes. *Yves St. Laurent Rive Gauche*, fashionable perfumeries, and chic cafés add to the atmosphere of the St-Sulpice neighborhood.

CHEZ DIANE

Oeufs Coques à la Purée de Morilles
Soft-Boiled Eggs with Morels

Coquilles Saint-Jacques à la Fondue d'Endives
Scallops with Endives

Crème Caramel à l'Orange
Orange Caramel Cream

Oeufs Coques à la Purée de Morilles

Soft-Boiled Eggs with Morels

This appetizer is served with strips of toast for dipping into the eggs. A Cabernet such as Bourgueil or a Beaujolais such as Brouilly is good alongside.

1 ounce (30 g) dried morel mushrooms

½ teaspoon butter

1 small shallot, minced

3 tablespoons dry white wine

1 teaspoon tomato paste

Salt and freshly ground black pepper to taste

8 eggs

8 slices sandwich bread, toasted and cut into thin strips

Soak the dried mushrooms in warm water for 1 hour. Gently squeeze dry and chop finely.

In a small saucepan, melt the butter over medium heat and sauté the shallot for 2 minutes, or until translucent. Pour in the wine and bring to a boil. Stir in the morels, tomato paste, salt, and pepper. Reduce heat to low and simmer for about 30 minutes, stirring occasionally. Set aside and keep warm.

Bring a medium saucepan of water to a boil, add the eggs, and immediately lower the heat so the water is barely simmering. Cook the eggs for 3 minutes. Using a slotted spoon, remove the eggs and run under cold water.

Using a sharp knife, neatly slice off the tops of the eggs and reserve the tops intact. Place each egg in an egg cup, top with a spoonful of the morel mixture, and cover with an egg top set on a slant. Place 2 egg cups on each of 4 plates and serve with the strips of toast.

Makes 4 servings

CHEZ DIANE

Coquilles St-Jacques
à la Fondue d'Endives

Scallops with Endives

Scallops and endives is a classic bistro pairing. A glass of Sancerre Blanc, Jurançon, or Sauvignon Blanc makes an excellent accompaniment.

- 3 tablespoons plus ½ cup (4 oz/125 g) butter, cut into ¼-inch (6-mm) slices

- 4 Belgian endives, trimmed, halved lengthwise, and sliced crosswise

- Salt and freshly ground black pepper to taste

- 12 sea scallops

- Juice of ½ fresh lemon

- 1 tablespoon crème fraîche (see Basics)

- ½ bunch chives, chopped, for garnish

In a large sauté pan or skillet, melt 2 tablespoons of the butter over medium-low heat and add the endives. Sprinkle with salt and pepper and sauté gently for 5 minutes, or until the endives are tender; set aside.

Season the scallops with salt and pepper to taste. In a large sauté pan or skillet, melt 1 tablespoon of the butter over medium-high heat and sauté the scallops for 2 minutes on each side, or until golden brown.

In a small, heavy saucepan, bring the lemon juice to a boil and whisk in the ½ cup (4 oz/125 g) butter one piece at a time. Remove from heat, whisk in the crème fraîche, and season lightly with salt and pepper.

To serve, divide the endive slices among 4 shallow soup bowls or dinner plates. Arrange 5 scallops on top of each serving. Spoon the lemon butter over, sprinkle with the chopped chives, and serve immediately.

Makes 4 servings

Crème Caramel à l'Orange

Orange Caramel Cream

Caramel

¾ cup (6 oz/175 g) sugar

Grated zest and juice of 2 oranges

3 eggs

3 egg yolks

¾ cup (6 oz/175 g) sugar

Juice of 2 oranges

2 cups (16 fl oz/500 ml) milk

1½ tablespoons Grand Marnier

To make the caramel: In a small, heavy saucepan, bring the sugar to a boil over medium-high heat. Cook without stirring until the sugar turns golden brown, about 5 minutes. Immediately pour into six ½-cup (4 fl oz/125 ml) custard cups or ramekins, tilting the ramekins in all directions to partially coat the sides. Sprinkle the orange zest evenly over the caramel; set the cups or ramekins aside.

Preheat the oven to 400°F (200°C). In a medium bowl, combine the eggs, egg yolks, sugar, orange juice, milk, and Grand Marnier; stir until thoroughly blended.

Pour the custard into the prepared custard cups or ramekins. Transfer them to a baking dish and fill the dish with hot water to come halfway up the sides of the cups or ramekins. Bake in the preheated oven for 35 minutes, or until a knife inserted in the center of a custard comes out clean. Let cool and refrigerate until serving time.

Makes 6 custards

LA FONTAINE DE MARS

When current *patronne* Christiane Boudon first saw La Fontaine de Mars, she was the manager of a large American restaurant in Paris. Perhaps it was the bistro's intimate size or possibly its intrinsic French character, but in any case, it was love at first sight, or as the French say, *un coup de foudre.* Madame Boudon decided this bistro was for her! At the time, La Fontaine had been owned and managed by Paul and Andrée Launey for sixty years, and it took four more years for Christiane to persuade the couple to sell her their picture-perfect establishment.

Like the Launeys, Madame Boudon is from the Pyrénées and her menu is almost entirely based on the cuisine of that region. Excellent specialties include the bistro's cassoulet and Tarte au Poire Bourdaloue (page 104). The extensive wine list includes full-bodied Cahors wine from the Pyrénées, and Lillet, a delicious wine-based aperitif from southwest France.

Originally a *café-charbon*, where locals could stop for a quick glass of wine or bite to eat when they bought coal for their stoves, La Fontaine de Mars is named for the large fountain topped by a statue of the god Mars in the tiny plaza next door. Long before the bistro existed, Napoleon's horses were watered at this fountain. Although Jacques and Christiane Boudon have refurbished their bistro, they have carefully preserved the main dining room's charming early-twentieth-century decor. Once you push through the heavy velvet curtains at the entrance, you'll see the same lace café curtains, red and white checkered table linens, zinc bar near the back, and carefully handwritten menus that the bistro's patrons have enjoyed for decades.

NEIGHBORHOOD WALK

The Eiffel Tower, Paris's most recognizable monument, is only a five-minute walk from La Fontaine de Mars. Despite the fame of its sillouette, most Paris visitors are awestruck at their first sight of this belle-époque structure. There's nothing like the feeling of standing directly beneath the tower and looking up at its beautiful filigree arches. Designed by Gustave Eiffel for the Universal Exhibition in 1889, the Tour Eiffel stands almost one thousand feet tall and is made from more than seven thousand tons of iron. Stairs and an elevator lead up to the first and second platforms, where there are restaurants, bars, and gift stores. The third platform, accessible by elevator only, offers a spectacular view of the city.

Between the Eiffel Tower and the Ecole Militaire is the Champs de Mars, a park composed of gardens in both the formal French and the more casual English styles. Across the Seine, there is a terraced garden at place du Trocadéro with a stunning view of the Champs de Mars and the Eiffel Tower. The Palais de Chaillot, which was constructed at Trocadéro for the Paris Exhibition of 1937, now houses the Maritime Museum and the Musée de l'Homme, a museum devoted to the history of mankind.

LA FONTAINE DE MARS

Petits Pâtés de Cèpes

Little Mushroom Pâtés

Poulet Fermier aux Morilles

Free-Range Chicken with Morel Sauce

Tarte au Poire Bourdaloue

Bordeaux-Style Pear Tart

Petits Pâtés de Cèpes

Little Mushroom Pâtés

Serve these warm, with French bread and a small green salad dressed with a mild vinaigrette.

2 tablespoons peanut oil

10 ounces (315 g) cèpe, porcini, or morel mushrooms, chopped

10 ounces (315 g) white mushrooms

1 tablespoon butter

1 garlic clove, minced

½ bunch chives, chopped

1 tablespoon heavy cream

1 whole egg

2 egg yolks

½ tablespoon minced fresh parsley

Salt and freshly ground black pepper to taste

Butter four 3-inch-diameter (7.5-cm) ovenproof ramekins. Preheat the oven to 350°F (180°C).

In a medium sauté pan or skillet over medium heat, heat the peanut oil and sauté all the mushrooms for 5 minutes. Transfer the mushrooms to a colander and drain. In the same pan melt the butter over medium heat and sauté the mushrooms again until they are lightly browned and all the moisture has evaporated. Add the garlic and chives and sauté for 2 minutes. Remove from heat and set aside to cool.

In a medium bowl, whisk the cream, egg, egg yolks, and parsley together until thoroughly blended. Stir in the mushrooms until thoroughly blended. Season with salt and pepper. Pour into the prepared ramekins and bake in the preheated oven for 40 minutes, or until the tops are crusty and a knife inserted in the center of a pâté comes out clean.

Remove the pâtés from the oven and let cool to room temperature. Unmold the pâtés and serve.

Makes 4 servings

LA FONTAINE DE MARS

Poulet Fermier aux Morilles

Free-Range Chicken with Morel Sauce

Serve with basmati rice and fresh artichoke hearts or peas.

Court Bouillon

2½ quarts (2.5 l) water

1 carrot, peeled and chopped

1 onion, chopped

1 clove

Bouquet garni: 1 parsley sprig, 1 thyme sprig,
   and 1 bay leaf tied in a cheesecloth square

3 tablespoons coarse sea salt

One 4-pound (2-kg) free-range chicken,
   cleaned and trussed with kitchen string

2 tablespoons butter

1 shallot, finely diced

14 ounces (440 g) morel mushrooms, sliced

⅔ cup (5 fl oz/160 ml) veal stock (see Basics)
   or canned low-salt beef broth

1½ cups (12 fl oz/375 ml) heavy cream

Salt and freshly ground black pepper to taste

To make the court bouillon: In a large pot or stockpot over medium heat,
combine all the court bouillon ingredients. Bring to a boil, reduce heat, and
simmer for 20 minutes. Put the chicken in the pot and bring to a boil.
Reduce heat, cover, and simmer for about 1 hour.

In a medium saucepan, melt the butter over medium-low heat and sauté
the shallot for 3 minutes, or until translucent. Add the morels and sauté for
15 minutes. Pour in the stock or broth and 1 cup (8 fl oz/250 ml) of the court
bouillon; cook for 10 minutes. Pour in the cream and cook for 5 minutes, or

until the liquid is slightly reduced. Season with salt and pepper.

Remove the chicken from the sauce and drain. Cut the chicken into serving pieces and slice the breast. Arrange the chicken on each of 4 plates and spoon the morel sauce over. Serve warm.

Makes 4 servings

Tarte au Poire Bourdaloue

Bordeaux-Style Pear Tart

This rich pear and frangipane tart makes a lovely fall or winter dessert. Frangipane is a sweet almond cream said to have been invented by the Italian perfumer Frangipani, who lived in Paris during the reign of Louis XIII.

1½ cups (12 oz/375 g) sugar

4 cups (1 l) water

4 large pears

6 tablespoons (3 oz/90g) butter at room temperature

1½ cups (4 oz/130 g) ground blanched almonds

½ cup (4 oz/125 g) sugar

2 eggs

1 cup (8 fl oz/250 ml) pastry cream (see Basics)

3 tablespoons rum

One 9-inch (23-cm) partially-baked Pâte Sablée shell (see Basics)

¼ cup (1½ oz/45 g) slivered almonds

In a medium saucepan, combine the sugar and water and bring to a simmer over medium heat until the sugar dissolves; remove from heat. Peel, halve, and core the pears. Add the pears to the sugar syrup and poach them over low heat until tender when pierced with a sharp knife, about 10 minutes; keep just below simmering, as an actual simmer may cause the fruit to burst.

Preheat the oven to 350°F (180°C). In a bowl, beat the butter until pale and fluffy. Beat in the ground almonds, sugar, and eggs until thoroughly mixed. Gradually blend in the pastry cream and rum. Stir until thoroughly blended.

Pour the mixture into the partially baked tart shell. Top with the poached pears, cored side down and narrow end facing the center. Sprinkle with the almonds and bake in the preheated oven for 40 minutes, or until a knife inserted in the custard comes out almost clean; do not overcook. Let cool to room temperature before serving.

Makes one 9-inch (23-cm) tart; serves 8

LA GARGOTE

351 PLACE D'YOUVILLE, MONTRÉAL, QUÉBEC H2Y 2B7

Monsieur Jean-Pierre Ousset established La Gargote on Valentine's Day, 1996. The bistro is situated in the heart of old Montréal in a neighborhood that recalls the style and charm of Europe. According to the restaurant's own definition, a *gargote* is a small neighborhood restaurant with unpretentious, reasonably priced cuisine. While staying true to the meaning of its name, this bistro distinguishes itself with enticing cuisine inspired by Provence.

La Gargote operates according to a *table d'hôte* formula: a prix fixe menu with several choices that change daily and make use of the freshest possible seasonal ingredients. A small à la carte menu of tempting, carefully prepared dishes is also available.

Monsieur Ousset, the bistro's friendly proprietor, graciously welcomes guests in a dining room with a relaxed, convivial atmosphere. With its stone walls, wooden ceiling, sunny terrace for summer, and a cozy working fireplace for winter, La Gargote wins the heart of all who visit.

LA GARGOTE

Calmars Frits à la Provençale
Fried Calamari with Provençal Sauce

Confit de Canard aux Figues Confites
Duck Confit with Figs

Crème Catalane aux Framboises
Catalán Cream with Raspberries

Calmars Frits à la Provençale

Fried Calamari with Provençal Sauce

A lively starter for a Provence-inspired bistro dinner.

Provençal Sauce

1 tablespoon plus ¾ cup (6 fl oz/180 ml) olive oil

6 tomatoes, quartered

1 fresh rosemary sprig

4 garlic cloves, crushed

Salt and freshly ground black pepper to taste

2 pounds (1 kg) squid, cleaned and rinsed

Flour for dredging

2 cups (16 fl oz/500 ml) peanut or corn oil

2 lemons, quartered, for garnish

To make the sauce: In a medium sauté pan or skillet, heat the 1 tablespoon oil over medium heat and add the tomatoes, rosemary, garlic, salt, and pepper. Bring to a simmer, cover, and cook for 20 minutes. Remove the rosemary sprig.

Transfer the sauce to a blender or food processor. With the machine running, gradually pour in the ¾ cup (6 fl oz/180 ml) olive oil in a thin stream until the sauce emulsifies. Set aside.

Cut the squid into ¼-inch-thick (6-mm) rings; pat dry with paper towels. Dredge the squid in flour, shaking off any excess.

In a Dutch oven or deep-fat fryer over high heat, heat the oil to 375°F (190°C), or until almost smoking. Add the squid to the oil in batches and cook for 3 to 4 minutes, or until golden brown. Using a slotted spoon, transfer to paper towels. Season with salt and pepper. Serve on 6 individual plates, garnished with a lemon wedge. Serve the sauce alongside.

Makes 6 servings

Following: Calmars Frits à la Provençale

Confit de Canard aux Figues Confites

Duck Confit with Figs

The tradition of cooking and storing duck in its own fat goes back to the Moors, who passed through southwest France in the eighth century A.D. Once a means of preserving meat over long periods of time, today this technique is prized for the intense flavor it produces. This recipe should be started at least 2 days before serving.

6 whole duck legs (thighs and drumsticks)

¼ cup (2 oz/60 g) coarse sea salt or kosher salt

Freshly ground black pepper to taste

½ teaspoon ground nutmeg

1 garlic clove, minced

6 fresh thyme sprigs

3 bay leaves

2 pounds (1 kg) rendered duck fat, (see Resources) cut into pieces

Fig Sauce

⅓ cup (3 fl oz/80 ml) water

¼ cup (2 oz/60 g) sugar

½ cup (4 fl oz/125 ml) white wine vinegar

Julienned zest of 1 orange (see Basics)

1 tomato, quartered

2 cups (16 fl oz/500 ml) beef stock (see Basics) or canned low-salt beef broth

Salt to taste

3 to 4 peppercorns

⅔ cup (5 fl oz/160 ml) ruby port

12 fresh figs, halved or quartered

1 tablespoon butter

Sautéed apples for serving (see Basics)

Rub the duck legs with the salt, pepper, and nutmeg. Place the legs in a shallow glass dish and top each leg with some of the garlic, a thyme sprig, and half a bay leaf. Cover with plastic wrap and refrigerate overnight.

Cut the duck legs in half to separate the thighs and drumsticks. In a large, heavy pot, melt the duck fat. Place the meat, thyme, garlic, and bay leaves in the melted fat. Bring to a boil, then reduce heat and simmer, uncovered, until the meat is easily pierced with a fork and the juices run clear, about 1 hour.

Using tongs, carefully transfer the meat to a deep earthenware bowl or ceramic terrine. Strain the fat through a fine-meshed sieve. Pour the fat over the duck to completely cover the meat. Let cool until the fat hardens; make sure the duck pieces are totally sealed in the fat so that no air can reach them. Cover and refrigerate for at least 24 hours or up to 3 weeks.

Preheat the oven to 450°F (230°C). Remove the duck legs from the fat, scraping off as much of the excess fat as possible. Place the meat, skin-side down, in a baking pan. Bake in the preheated oven until the skin is crispy and the meat is heated through, about 15 minutes.

Meanwhile, make the sauce: In a medium, heavy saucepan, boil the water and sugar until a light caramel color. Immediately remove from heat and add the vinegar, orange zest, tomato, stock or broth, salt, and peppercorns. Cook over high heat until reduced by half. Add the port and boil for 2 minutes. Season with salt and pepper. Strain through a fine-meshed sieve, pressing the tomato through with the back of a spoon. Stir in the figs. Swirl in the butter until the sauce is shiny.

Preheat the broiler. Arrange the duck pieces on a broiler tray and broil to brown the skins. Spoon some of the fig sauce on each of 6 plates and top with a duck leg and thigh and a serving of sautéed apples.

Makes 6 servings

Crème Catalane aux Framboises

Catalán Cream with Raspberries

A smooth and silky custard with a crisp sugar topping. Start preparations the day before serving.

5 egg yolks

1 tablespoon flour

⅓ cup (3 fl oz/80 ml) milk

½ cup (4 fl oz/125 ml) heavy cream

Meringue

5 egg whites

⅔ cup (5 oz/155 g) sugar

½ cup (4 fl oz/125 ml) water

1½ cups (6 oz/185 g) fresh raspberries

6 tablespoons (3 oz/90 g) packed brown sugar

In a medium bowl, whisk the egg yolks until pale. Whisk in the flour and milk until smooth.

In a medium saucepan, heat the cream over medium-high heat until bubbles form around the edges of the pan. Gradually whisk the hot cream into the egg mixture. Return the mixture to the saucepan and bring to a boil over medium heat, whisking constantly. Reduce heat to a simmer and whisk for 2 to 3 minutes; remove from heat.

In a large bowl, beat the egg whites until stiff, glossy peaks form; set aside. In a small saucepan, bring the sugar and water to a boil and cook until syrupy but not colored. Remove from heat and pour in a thin stream into the egg whites, whisking constantly. Fold the meringue mixture into the cream mixture.

Divide the raspberries among 6 individual ramekins and fill each ramekin with the custard. Cover and refrigerate for at least 12 hours before serving.

Just before serving, preheat the broiler. Place 1 tablespoon of the brown sugar in a fine-meshed sieve and push the sugar through with the back of a spoon to evenly layer the top of a custard. Repeat with the remaining custards. Place the custards under the broiler about 2 inches from the heat source until the sugar is melted and crisp, about 30 seconds to 1 minute, being careful not to burn. Let cool for a few minutes and serve.

Makes 6 custards

CHEZ GERMAINE

30, RUE PIERRE-LEROUX, 75007 PARIS

MÉTRO VANEAU OR DUROC

Chez Germaine is an unpretentious family-style bistro tucked away on a quiet street just off bustling rue de Sevres in one of Paris's wealthiest neighborhoods. The bistro's seven tables, set within centimeters of each other and covered with paper place mats, are crowded with satisfied diners enjoying true *cuisine de grand-mère*—the kind of food you'd expect to be served in a French grandmother's kitchen. Specialties include the house pâté and warm clafoutis, a traditional French dessert made with seasonal fruits. Diners can choose from a very reasonably priced prix fixe menu that includes an appetizer, main dish, and dessert, or order specialties à la carte. Chez Germaine is one of the few nonsmoking restaurants in Paris.

Madame Germaine Babkine opened Chez Germaine on July 14, 1954. Thirty-eight years later to the day, she was succeeded by Ingrid Blakely. Thanks to Madame Blakely's generosity and the experience of waitress Colette and chef Pierre, both of whom have worked at Chez Germaine since the 1960s, the bistro's warm-hearted atmosphere and classic cooking have continued unchanged.

Chez Germaine is almost always packed for both lunch and dinner, so it's essential to make reservations. Madame Blakely and her chef shop daily to make sure everything they serve is fresh, and it's not uncommon for them to simply run out of food by the end of the evening! In order to serve as many people as possible, patrons are sometimes seated next to strangers and often find themselves making friends by the end of a delicious meal. In some ways, this is the epitome of bistro style—a place where neighborhood regulars, students, and families come together to enjoy good food and lively company.

NEIGHBORHOOD WALK

Chez Germaine's neighborhood is a shopper's heaven. The stores along nearby rues de Babylone, de Sevres and du Cherche-Midi are a treasure trove of almost all the necessities of chic Parisian existence. You'll find chocolate boutiques elegant enough to be jewelry stores, a flower shop devoted exclusively to roses, the perfect place to buy exquisite stationery, designer shoe stores, and magnificent selections of charcuterie and cheeses. The store windows seem to glow with beautiful objects, and the sidewalks bustle with Parisians going about their daily lives. One gourmet landmark definitely worth visiting is Poilâne, at 8, rue du Cherche-Midi. This is the most famous bakery in Paris and its round loaves of crusty sourdough bread, *sablés* (thin butter cookies), and scrumptious apple tarts are not to be missed. Be sure to ask to visit the bakery's ancient stone cellar, which houses Poilâne's large wood-burning ovens.

Also in the neighborhood is Au Bon Marché, a typical Parisian department store. La Grande Epicerie, on the ground floor, is one of the largest grocery stores in the city, and a wonderful place to find gourmet goodies *à la française*.

CHEZ GERMAINE

Terrine Fermière Maison
Country-Style Pâté

Saumon à la Fondue de Poireaux
Salmon with Leek Sauce

Sauté de Veau
Veal Stew

Clafoutis aux Fruits
Fruit Clafoutis

Terrine Fermière Maison

Country-Style Pâté

Pâté, the prelude to many a bistro meal, is served with crusty bread, Dijon mustard, and cornichons. Accompany with a light red wine, such as a Beaujolais or Zinfandel, or a dry white wine.

1 pound (500 g) ground pork shoulder

12 ounces (375 g) pork liver

8 ounces (250 g) pork loin

3 large onions, coarsely chopped

Salt and freshly ground black pepper to taste

1 pound sheets of caul fat or blanched bacon slices (see Basics) for wrapping the pâté

Preheat the oven to 350°F (180°C). In a food processor, process the ground pork, liver, loin, onions, salt, and pepper for 2 minutes, or until blended but still chunky. Line the bottom and sides of a 9½-by-3½-by-3½-inch (24-by-9-by-9-cm) terrine or a 9-by-5-inch (23-by-13-cm) loaf pan with half of the caul fat or bacon slices, layering the bacon crosswise. Add the pâté mixture. Cover with a layer of caul fat or lengthwise bacon strips, pressing down firmly with your hands.

Cover the terrine or loaf pan with a lid or aluminum foil and transfer to a baking pan. Add hot water to the baking pan to come halfway up the sides of the terrine or loaf pan. Bake in the preheated oven for 2 hours, or until the juices run clear.

Remove the pâté pan from the oven, uncover, and drain off the liquid. Place a piece of foil-wrapped cardboard over the pâté and top with a 2-pound (1-kg) weight. Refrigerate for at least 8 hours or up to 2 days to let the pâté develop its full flavor. Cut serving slices right from the baking dish at the table, or unmold the pâté and peel off the fat or bacon slices. The pâté will keep in the refrigerator for about 10 days.

Serves 8 to 10

Saumon à la Fondue de Poireaux

Salmon with Leek Sauce

Serve with boiled or steamed potatoes and drink a Muscadet or Chardonnay.

3 tablespoons butter

3 leeks, white part only, finely chopped

5 shallots, minced

2 tablespoons flour

2 cups (16 fl oz/500 ml) fish stock (see Basics) or clam juice

⅓ cup (3 oz/80 ml) crème fraîche (see Basics)

Salt and ground white pepper to taste

Juice of 1 lemon

One 3-pound (1.5-kg) salmon fillet, skinned and boned,
or six 6-ounce salmon fillets, skinned and boned

In a sauté pan or skillet, melt 2 tablespoons of the butter over medium-low heat and sauté the leeks for 10 minutes, or until tender; set aside.

In a small sauté pan or skillet, melt the remaining 1 tablespoon butter over medium heat and sauté the shallots for 3 minutes, or until translucent. Sprinkle with the flour and stir for about 3 minutes. Gradually whisk in the fish stock or clam juice to make a smooth, creamy sauce. Stir in the crème fraîche, leeks, lemon juice, and salt and pepper; set aside and keep warm.

In a large sauté pan or skillet, bring about 3 inches (7.5 cm) water and a pinch of salt just to a simmer over medium-low heat. Add the salmon and poach for 8 to 10 minutes, or until springy to the touch. Using a slotted spatula, carefully remove the salmon and transfer to a large platter. Pour the leek sauce over and serve immediately.

Makes 6 servings

Sauté de Veau

Veal Stew

Serve with rice, a simple green salad, crusty French bread, and a red Bordeaux, rosé, or Zinfandel.

3 tablespoons butter

1 tablespoon olive oil

2 pounds (1 kg) veal stew meat, cut into 1-inch pieces

4 onions, diced, and 1 onion, studded with 4 cloves

2 tablespoons tomato paste

2 garlic cloves, minced

Bouquet garni: 1 parsley sprig, 1 thyme sprig, and 1 bay leaf, tied in a cheesecloth square

1 tablespoon flour

4 cups (1 l) veal stock (see Basics) or canned low-salt beef broth

⅔ cup (5 fl oz/160 ml) dry white wine

1 teaspoon coarse sea salt

½ teaspoon freshly ground black pepper

In a large, heavy pot over medium-high heat, melt 1 tablespoon of the butter with the olive oil and sauté the veal until browned on all sides, about 7 minutes. Using a slotted spoon, transfer the meat to a plate.

In a large, heavy saucepan melt the remaining 2 tablespoons butter over medium heat and sauté the diced onions until golden, about 5 minutes. Add the clove-studded onion, tomato paste, garlic, and bouquet garni. Sprinkle in the flour. Stir in the wine, stock or broth, salt, and pepper. Bring to a boil, skimming off any foam that rises to the surface. Reduce heat and simmer for 1 hour, stirring occasionally. Remove the bouquet garni and studded onion and serve.

Makes 8 servings

Opposite: Clafoutis (page 120)

CHEZ GERMAINE

Clafoutis aux Fruits

Fruit Clafoutis

A simple puddinglike dessert traditionally made with cherries, clafoutis is also delicious with prunes, sautéed apples, pears, or berries. If you like, dust powdered sugar over the warm clafoutis before serving.

7 tablespoons (3½ oz/105 g) sugar

3 tablespoons flour

½ teaspoon baking powder

¼ teaspoon baking soda

Pinch of salt

3 eggs, beaten

⅓ cup (3 fl oz/80 ml) milk

½ cup (4 oz/125 g) butter, melted

2 cups (8 oz/250 g) fruit such as pitted fresh Bing cherries or prunes, sautéed, diced apples, diced pears, or fresh raspberries or blackberries

Powdered sugar for dusting (optional)

Preheat the oven to 400°F (200°C). Butter and sugar a 9-inch (23-cm) pie plate.

In a medium bowl, stir the sugar, flour, baking powder, baking soda, salt, and eggs together. Gradually stir in the milk and butter until thoroughly blended.

Pour the batter into the prepared baking dish and arrange the fruit over the batter. Bake in the preheated oven for 25 minutes, or until puffed and golden brown. Let cool slightly, sprinkle with powdered sugar, if desired, and serve warm.

Makes 6 to 8 servings

RESTAURANT DE LA GRILLE

80, RUE DU FAUBOURG-POISSONNIÈRE, 75010 PARIS
MÉTRO POISSONNIÈRE

Yves and Geneviève Cullère have been the proud owners of La Grille since 1971. They serve an elegant *cuisine bourgeoise* to crowds of regulars, some of whom have been patronizing the bistro for over twenty years. Many diners from the bistro's early years now bring in their children, and even grandchildren, to enjoy Yves's cooking and Geneviève's warmth and hospitality. Madame Cullère's own collection of antique laces decorates La Grille's burgundy velvet banquettes and carved, dark wooden walls, and her collection of antique hats serves as a reminder of the days when ladies and gentlemen always wore hats and placed them for safe-keeping on the brass racks that encircle the dining room. In pre-revolutionary France, this building housed a corner cabaret that was frequented by fishmongers on their way from Dieppe to Les Halles, Paris's central market. Named for the wrought-iron grilles protecting its windows and doors, La Grille was transformed over the years into a restaurant. Today thanks to the Cullères, the bistro has a glowing reputation for excellent cuisine. Suitably enough, chef Cullère specializes in seafood, and his Turbot Grillé avec Beurre Blanc (page 130) is ranked by critics as among the best in Paris. Fresh seafood is still brought in every day from Dieppe, and Bernard, a Scotsman who supplies fish to some of Paris's best restaurants, is a favorite patron at La Grille.

It's clear that despite the hard work and long hours entailed in running their bistro (chef Cullère starts work at four o'clock every morning!), La Grille is a labor of love for the couple. Visiting their establishment is like being invited to join in as they *faire la fête*, or celebrate with family and friends.

NEIGHBORHOOD WALK

A twenty-minute walk north of La Grille takes you to the Montmartre district, where artists, writers, and free-thinkers congregated throughout the nineteenth and early twentieth centuries. Emile Zola, Toulouse-Lautrec, George Sand, and Mary Cassat were among the famous Parisians who frequented the area's famed cafés and cabarets.

Montmartre's nickname is *"la butte,"* which means hill or mound, and steep streets, stone staircases, and views of the city are hallmarks of this particular corner of Paris. An easy way to make the ascent is to take the funicular, or tram, from the top of rue de Steinkerque, a narrow street lined with shops selling tourist baubles, clothing, and bolts of colorful fabrics. The funicular arrives right in front of the imposing nineteenth-century Sacré-Cœur basilica, whose majestic white domes seem to watch over all of Paris. Although Montmartre is no longer a hotbed of artistic and intellectual activity, visitors will enjoy its villagelike charm.

The tenth arrondissement itself, where La Grille is located, is home to two major train stations, Gare de l'Est and Gare du Nord. Just south of La Grille is the delightfully named rue du Paradis, famous for its crystal and porcelain shops. The Baccarat museum is at 30 bis, rue du Paradis.

RESTAURANT DE LA GRILLE

Terrine de l'Océan

Seafood Terrine

Galette de Pommes de Terre

Sautéed Potato Pancake

Turbot Grillé avec Beurre Blanc

Grilled Turbot with White Butter Sauce

Tarte aux Fruits Frais

Fresh-Berry Tart

Terrine de l'Océan

Seafood Terrine

Perfect for an elegant buffet or a formal dinner, this superb terrine is time-consuming but worth the effort. Begin preparations the day before you plan to serve. Chef Cullère brought this recipe to his bistro in Paris from his native Nantes on the Atlantic Coast.

1½ pounds (750 g) sole or pike fillets

1 pound (500 g) salmon fillets

1½ pounds (750 g) ocean perch or mullet fillet

1 pound (500 g) fish bones

One 1-pound (500-g) live lobster

4 tablespoons (2 oz/60 g) unsalted butter

2 tablespoons Cognac or brandy

1 cup (8 fl oz/250 ml) water

2 pounds (1 kg) mussels, scrubbed and debearded

1 pound leeks, white part only, chopped (green tops chopped, washed, and reserved)

4 shallots, finely chopped

2 garlic cloves, minced

8 ounces (250 g) sorrel or spinach, stemmed and finely chopped

Leaves from 1 bunch fresh tarragon, minced

1 teaspoon salt

¼ teaspoon freshly ground black pepper

¾ teaspoon quatre épices*

2 teaspoons Dijon mustard

3 large eggs, beaten

1 pound bacon, blanched (see Basics)

1 egg white, beaten until frothy

10 ounces (315 g) sea scallops, rinsed

1 envelope plain gelatin

Herb Mayonnaise

1 cup (8 oz/250 g) mayonnaise

1 tablespoon capers, drained and chopped

2 tablespoons minced mixed fresh herbs

Remove all the skin and bones from the fish fillets; put the skin and the 1 pound (500 g) of fish bones in a large pot. Arrange all the fillets on a baking sheet, separating each kind of fish.

Using a large, sharp knife, kill the lobster instantly by making an incision in the back of the shell where the chest and tail meet. Separate the claws from the body. Shell the lobster and remove the meat, reserving the carcass.

In a large sauté pan or skillet, melt 2 tablespoons of the butter over medium-high heat and sauté the lobster pieces for 3 minutes. Pour in the Cognac or brandy and carefully ignite with a long-handled match. Shake the pan until the flames subside. Remove from heat and let the lobster cool to the touch.

Remove the lobster meat from the tail and claws and set aside with the fish fillets. Place the lobster carcass in the pot with the fish skin and bones.

In a large pot, bring the water to a boil. Add the mussels, cover, and cook for 5 minutes, or until the mussels open; discard any that do not open. Strain the liquid through a cheesecloth-lined sieve into the pot with the fish skin. Shell the mussels and set them aside. Add the green leek tops to the pot with the fish skin and bones.

In a small sauté pan or skillet, melt the remaining 2 tablespoons butter over medium heat and sauté the chopped leek whites, shallots, and garlic for 5 minutes, or until the leeks are soft but not browned.

In a blender or food processor, combine the fillets and lobster meat and process for 1 minute. Pour the mixture into a large bowl. Add the cooked vegetables, sorrel or spinach, tarragon, salt, pepper, quatre épices, and mustard; stir until thoroughly blended. Stir in the eggs and fold in the cooked mussels.

Preheat the oven to 400°F (200°C). Line a 9-by-5-inch (23-by-13-cm) loaf pan with the bacon slices, arranging them crosswise so they overhang the sides. Brush the bacon with the egg white.

Spread one fourth of the fish mixture in the bottom of the terrine. Add an even layer of half of the fillets. Cover with another fourth of the fish mixture and then a layer of the scallops. Top with another fourth of the fish mixture, add the remaining fillets, and finish with a final layer of the fish mixture. Fold the bacon slices over the top and cover with the remaining bacon placed lengthwise.

Place the loaf pan in a baking pan and add hot water to come halfway up the sides of the loaf pan. Bake in the preheated oven for 1 hour and 15 minutes. Remove the terrine and invert onto a wire rack over a pan to drain. Let cool completely.

Run a knife around the edges of the mold and invert onto a plate with a sharp downward movement to unmold the terrine. Remove the bacon slices and discard. Return the terrine to the loaf pan, cover with plastic wrap, and refrigerate.

Add water to cover to the pot with the fish skin and bones. Bring to a boil, reduce heat to low, and simmer for 1 hour; strain and discard the solids. In a saucepan, boil the liquid until it reduces to 2 cups. Sprinkle in the gelatin and stir for 5 minutes, or until completely dissolved. Place the saucepan in bowl of ice, stirring occasionally, until the liquid is syrupy. Pour into the terrine to completely cover. Cover with plastic wrap and refrigerate overnight.

To make the herb mayonnaise: In a small bowl, stir together all the ingredients until thoroughly blended.

To serve, briefly dip the terrine into hot water and invert onto a serving platter. Using a sharp knife, slice the terrine, dipping the knife into boiling water after each slice. Serve with the herb mayonnaise.

Makes 16 servings

*$\frac{1}{8}$ teaspoon ground white pepper, $\frac{1}{4}$ teaspoon ground ginger, $\frac{1}{4}$ teaspoon ground nutmeg, $\frac{1}{8}$ teaspoon ground cloves

RESTAURANT DE LA GRILLE

Galette de Pommes de Terre

Sautéed Potato Pancake

Typically served with beef bourguignon, steaks, or roast chicken, this golden potato cake is easy to prepare.

4 ounces (125 g) slab bacon, cut into 1-by-¼-inch (2.5-cm-by-6-mm) strips

½ cup (2 oz/60 g) finely sliced onion

2 pounds (1 kg) potatoes, peeled and thinly sliced

4 tablespoons (2 fl oz/60 ml) peanut oil

Salt and freshly ground black pepper to taste

In a large skillet over medium heat, sauté the bacon until browned and crisp. Using a slotted spoon, transfer to paper towels to drain. Let cool and crumble.

Add the onion to the pan and sauté for 5 minutes, or until soft but not browned. Using a slotted spoon, remove the onion from the pan and set aside. Drain the bacon fat from the pan.

In a large bowl, toss the potatoes with 2 tablespoons of the peanut oil, the salt, and pepper; toss until well coated. Mix in the crumbled bacon and onion.

Heat the same pan used to cook the bacon over medium heat. Add the potato mixture, cover, and cook, shaking the pan occasionally, for about 20 minutes, or until the bottom of the pancake is browned.

Slide the potato pancake onto a platter. Heat the remaining 2 table-spoons peanut oil in the skillet over medium heat. Invert the plate over the pan to return the potato pancake. Cover and cook, shaking the pan occasionally, for 20 minutes, or until browned on the second side.

Slide the potato cake onto a heated serving platter. Cut into wedges and serve immediately.

Makes 6 servings

Opposite: Turbot Grillé (page 130)

Turbot Grillé avec Beurre Blanc

Grilled Turbot with White Butter Sauce

This dish is the specialty of the house at La Grille, and it is ranked by many critics as the best version in Paris. Serve with a Chavignol, Sancerre, or Sauvignon Blanc.

Sauce

½ cup (4 fl oz/125 ml) white wine vinegar

¼ cup (2 fl oz/60 ml) dry white wine

2 shallots, minced

1 tablespoon crème fraîche (see Basics)

7 tablespoons (3½ oz/105 g) unsalted butter at room temperature

Salt to taste

1½ pounds (750 g) turbot, sole, or orange roughy fillets,
   or 1 large whole gray sole

Salt and ground white pepper to taste

1 tablespoon unsalted butter

1 tablespoon vegetable oil

⅓ cup (¾ oz/20 g) dry bread crumbs

To make the sauce: In a small saucepan, combine the vinegar, wine, and shallots and boil to reduce to 1 tablespoon. Transfer the liquid to a double boiler over simmering water. Whisk in the crème fraiche and butter 1 table-spoon at a time. Remove from heat and season with salt. Strain the sauce through a fine-meshed sieve; set aside and keep warm over lukewarm water.

    Preheat the broiler. Arrange the fish fillets on a broiling tray and sea-son with salt and pepper. In a small saucepan, melt the butter with the oil. Brush this mixture over both sides of the fish fillets. Lightly coat the fish on both sides with the bread crumbs. Place the fish 3 to 4 inches (7.5 cm to 10 cm) from the heat source and broil for 5 to 8 minutes, or until the fish is opaque. Transfer the fish to a heated serving platter and serve immediately, with the white butter sauce.

Makes 4 servings

Tarte aux Fruits Frais

Fresh-Berry Tart

Mixed fresh berries, such as raspberries, strawberries, and blueberries, are
served simply in a prebaked pastry shell spread with crème fraîche.

One 9-inch (23-cm) baked Pâte Sucrée shell (see Basics)

2 cups (6 oz/500 g) crème fraîche (see Basics)

3 cups (12 oz/375 g) mixed fresh berries, such as raspberries,
strawberries, and blueberries

⅓ cup (3 oz/90 g) strawberry jam thinned with kirsch for glazing

Toasted sliced almonds for garnish

Spread the tart shell with the crème fraîche and top with the berries. Brush
the berries with the glaze. Sprinkle with the almonds.

Makes one 9-inch (23-cm) tart; serves 8

LE GRIZZLI

7, RUE ST-MARTIN, 75004 PARIS

MÉTRO HÔTEL-DE-VILLE OR CHÂTELET

Since its opening in 1902, Le Grizzli has steadfastly retained much of its original style and character. Of course, the real business of a bistro is its cuisine, and Le Grizzli offers nothing less than the best. Proprietor Bernard Arény was raised in the Pyrénées, and many of the recipes you'll find on the menu are from his native region. Specialties include smoked Auvergne ham and Croustade aux Pruneaux (page 140), which are often displayed on the sideboard in front of the bistro's bar.

Le Grizzli, like many bistros, has two dining rooms, one upstairs and one downstairs. The smaller downstairs room holds about seven tables and has soft cream-colored walls, large old-fashioned mirrors, and antique sconces that cast a golden glow in the evening. Dishes are sent to and from the kitchen in a turn-of-the-century dumbwaiter, which dates back to the bistro's early days. In fact, just about the only change Monsieur Arény has made to Le Grizzli's decor is the addition of his collection of posters, pictures, and flags with a bear motif. Originally the bistro was called Chez Jean, the name of its first proprietor. A subsequent owner decided to call the bistro Le Grizzli, in honor of the circus bears that used to perform nearby. Even though his grandfather's name is no longer on the bistro's facade, the original proprietor's grandson is a regular at Le Grizzli to this day.

At the turn of the century, Le Grizzli's neighborhood in the center of Paris was home to Les Halles, the huge open-air market that fed the capital city. Now, with Les Halles transformed into a large underground shopping mall, Le Grizzli's boisterous days are a thing of the past. Instead, an elegant clientele enjoys exceptional dishes from the Auvergne and the Pyrénées in a bistro that offers an old-fashioned mix of formality and friendliness.

NEIGHBORHOOD WALK

Located almost in the center of Paris, a few streets away from the Seine, Le Grizzli's old-fashioned elegance is worlds away from the modern-day hustle and bustle of rue St-Martin. Nearby place Igor Stravinski, the site of a circular fountain filled with colorful, moving figures by sculptors Jean Tinguely and Nikki de Saint-Phalle, is a favorite meeting place for locals and a great people-watching spot. Right beside the Stravinsky square is piazza Beaubourg, a wide sloping plaza in front of the Pompidou Center. The plaza is almost always crowded with tourists, caricaturists, street musicians, and groups of schoolchildren.

Built in the 1970s, Pompidou is one of the most popular tourist destinations in Paris. The steel and glass structure, with everything from escalators to heating ducts on the outside of its ultra-modern facade, still shocks Parisians and visitors alike. Besides housing France's world-class collection of twentieth-century art, the center also includes institutes for music and cultural development, a public library, and facilities for film and the performing arts. The neighborhood around the Pompidou center has been known as Beaubourg since the eleventh century, when it was a rural village outside the city limits. Now, its lovely seventeenth- and eighteenth-century houses stand in contrast to the crêpe stands and tourist stores on Beaubourg's pedestrian-only streets.

LE GRIZZLI

Marbré de Lentilles Vertes et Cocos
au Vinaigre de Xérès

Green Lentil and White Bean Terrine with Sherry Vinaigrette

Fricot de Veau aux Cèpes Séchés

Veal Stew with Dried Cèpe Mushrooms

Croustade aux Pruneaux à l'Armagnac

Pastry with Armagnac-Soaked Prunes

Marbré de Lentilles Vertes et Cocos au Vinaigre de Xérès

Green Lentil and White Bean Terrine with Sherry Vinaigrette

This cold first course is good for company, because it can be prepared completely ahead and sliced just before serving.

1 cup (7 oz/220 g) French green lentils (lentilles de Puy)

4 carrots, peeled and quartered

2 onions, cut in half

4 bay leaves

3 fresh thyme sprigs

8 ounces (250 g) slab bacon or smoked ham cut into small dice

Coarse sea salt and freshly ground black pepper to taste

1 cup (7 oz/220 g) dried Great Northern or navy beans, soaked in water overnight

3 envelopes plain gelatin

¼ cup (2 fl oz/60 ml) water

Vinaigrette

3 shallots, minced

1 teaspoon Dijon mustard

4 teaspoons sherry wine vinegar

1 cup (8 fl oz/250 ml) vegetable oil

½ bunch fresh chives, minced

Salt and freshly ground black pepper to taste

Minced hard-cooked egg whites and halved cherry tomatoes for garnish

Pick over and rinse the lentils. In a medium saucepan, combine the lentils, half of the carrots and onions, 2 of the bay leaves, 1 of the thyme sprigs, and half of the bacon or ham. Cover with cold water and bring to a boil. Reduce heat to low, cover, and simmer for 45 minutes. Season with salt and pepper and simmer 15 minutes more.

Meanwhile, in another medium saucepan, combine the beans and the remaining carrots, onion, bay leaves, thyme, and bacon or ham. Add salt and pepper to taste. Add cold water to cover and bring to a boil. Reduce heat to low, cover, and simmer for 45 minutes. Taste and adjust the seasoning and simmer 15 minutes more.

Strain the lentils and beans through a colander. Remove the onion and carrot and reserve all the cooking water. Combine the cooking water from the lentils with the water from the beans. Reserve 2 cups (16 fl oz/500 ml) of this liquid.

In a small saucepan, combine the gelatin and ¼ cup (2 fl oz/60 ml) water; let soak for 1 minute. Add the reserved cooking water and heat over low heat for 5 minutes, or until the gelatin is completely dissolved. Season with salt and pepper to taste.

In a large bowl, gently mix the lentils, beans, and gelatin mixture together. Pour into a 9-by-5-inch (23-by-13-cm) loaf pan. Cover with plastic wrap and refrigerate for 24 hours.

To make the vinaigrette: In a medium bowl, whisk together all the ingredients.

Just before serving, run a knife around the edges of the terrine and unmold. Cut into slices and serve covered with vinaigrette, sprinkled with egg white, and garnished with cherry tomatoes.

Makes about 12 servings

Fricot de Veau aux Cèpes Séchés

Veal Stew with Dried Cèpe Mushrooms

Proprietor Aręny suggests that you serve this lusty dish with steamed pota-toes and uncork a bottle of Cahors wine, or you could try an American Zinfandel or Pinot Noir. The dish can be prepared ahead to let the sauce mature in flavor.

8 ounces (250 g) dried cèpe or porcini mushrooms

2 cups (16 fl oz/500 ml) warm water

4 tablespoons (2 fl oz/60 ml) peanut oil

3 pounds (1.5 kg) veal stew meat, cut into 1-inch (2.5-cm) cubes

4 carrots, peeled and chopped

2 large onions, chopped

3 fresh thyme sprigs and bay leaves

Coarse sea salt and freshly ground black pepper to taste

¾ cup (6 fl oz/180 ml) dry white wine

6 cups (1.5 l) veal stock (see Basics) or canned low-salt beef broth

6 tablespoons (3 oz/90 g) butter

6 tablespoons (2 oz/60 g) flour

Soak the dried mushrooms in the warm water for 30 minutes. Rinse and squeeze dry. Strain the soaking liquid through a paper coffee filter and reserve. Chop the mushrooms.

In a large, heavy pan over medium-high heat, heat the oil and sauté the veal until evenly browned on all sides, about 7 minutes. Stir in the car-rots, onions, thyme, bay leaves, salt, and pepper. Pour in the white wine and cook to reduce the liquid by half. Add the mushrooms, reserved soak-ing liquid, and the stock or broth. Reduce heat to low and simmer for about 2 hours, or until the meat is very tender.

In a small, heavy saucepan, melt the butter over medium heat. Stir in the flour and cook, stirring constantly, for about 3 minutes. Gradually stir the flour mixture into the stew and cook, stirring frequently, until the sauce is smooth and thickened. Season with salt and pepper and serve hot.

Makes 6 servings

Croustade aux Pruneaux à l'Armagnac

Pastry with Armagnac-Soaked Prunes

A specialty of southwestern France, this tart highlights the sublime flavor of prunes soaked in Armagnac, a fine French brandy.

2 cups (12 oz/375 g) pitted prunes

4 cups (1 l) water

2 cups (16 oz/500 g) sugar

½ vanilla bean, split lengthwise, or 1 teaspoon vanilla extract

⅓ cup (3 fl oz/80 ml) Armagnac, Cognac, or brandy

1 pound (500 g) puff pastry (see Basics) or thawed frozen puff pastry

1½ cups (12 fl oz/375 ml) applesauce (see Basics)

1 egg, lightly beaten, for glazing

Powdered sugar for dusting

Vanilla ice cream for serving

Put the prunes in a medium bowl and add warm water to cover. Soak for 30 minutes; drain.

In a medium saucepan, combine the water, sugar, vanilla bean (if using), and Armagnac, Cognac, or brandy. Cook to reduce the liquid by one fourth. Pour over the prunes, cover, and refrigerate for 3 days.

Preheat the oven to 350°F (185°C). On a lightly floured work surface, roll the puff pastry out to a thickness of ¼ inch (6 mm). Cut the pastry into two 12-inch-diameter (30-cm) circles. Fit one of the circles into a 10-inch (25-cm) pie plate. Spread the applesauce over the pastry and top with an even layer of the prunes. Pour the prune liquid over. Cover with the second pastry circle and pinch the edges together. Using a brush, glaze the top of the tart with the beaten egg. Bake in the preheated oven for 45 minutes, or until the pastry is golden brown.

Dust with powdered sugar and serve warm, accompanied with a scoop of vanilla ice cream.

Makes one 10-inch (25-cm) tart; serves 8

RESTAURANT
MARIE-LOUISE

52, RUE CHAMPIONNET, 75018 PARIS
MÉTRO SIMPLON OR PORTE-DE-CLIGNANCOURT

Marie-Louise was established during the 1930s in a house near the Porte de Clingnancourt at the northern end of Paris. Starting in the 1960s, Monsieur and Madame Coillet presided over the bistro's classic kitchen and its two old-fashioned dining rooms. In 1997, they sold the bistro to Guy Roussel, an outgoing proprietor who satisfies devoted neighborhood regulars with generous portions of traditional bistro cuisine in surroundings reminiscent of another time. Yves Clémenceau, an old hand in the restaurant business, is now the *maître des lieux*, or manager of day-to-day operations. Marie-Louise's two intimate dining rooms are on two different floors and furnished with an authentic zinc bar, white table linens, heavy cutlery, and simple flowers on every table. There is a nonsmoking room.

Chef Claude Moniez's specialties are served with style and include Chicken Marie-Louise (page 146), *boeuf à la ficelle* (poached beef fillet), and for dessert a Crème Caramel (page 148) reputed to be one of the best in Paris.

NEIGHBORHOOD WALK

Located in the eighteenth arrondissement at the northern tip of Paris, Marie-Louise is definitely off the beaten tourist track. And yet, the Clignancourt neighborhood (named after the Porte de Clignancourt, one of the portals that leads from Paris onto the highway encircling the city) is very Parisian in its own way. Stores and restaurants in immigrant neighborhoods mix with traditional French *boulangeries* and *fromageries*. The streets are busy and everything seems to move at a slightly faster pace than in other parts of the city. On weekends, more than a square mile of antiques, clothing, and other treasures attracts hoards of people to Paris's famous flea market, the Marché aux Puces St-Ouen. The market is just outside the city boundary, north of the Clignancourt métro stop.

If you're interested in a brief excursion outside Paris, the lovely Basilique St-Denis, mausoleum for the kings of France, is a short métro or taxi ride away. Constructed during the twelfth and thirteenth centuries, St-Denis was one of the first Gothic cathedrals in France. Parts of the original basilica are still standing, along with more recent restorations.

RESTAURANT MARIE-LOUISE

Salade Marie-Louise

Salad Marie-Louise

Poularde Marie-Louise

Chicken Marie-Louise

Crème Caramel

Caramel Custard

Salade Marie-Louise

Salad Marie-Louise

4 unpeeled boiling potatoes

5 ounces (155 g) white mushrooms

2 celery stalks

1 large slice ham, about ½ inch (1 cm) thick

Mayonnaise

1 tablespoon Dijon mustard

Salt and ground white pepper to taste

1 egg yolk

1 cup peanut or canola oil

Salt and ground white pepper to taste

Minced fresh parsley for garnish

In a large pot of boiling salted water, cook the potatoes for 20 minutes, or until tender when pierced with a fork. Rinse in cold water. Peel the potatoes and cut into small dice.

Cut the mushrooms, celery, and ham into small dice. In a salad bowl, gently mix the mushrooms, celery, ham, and potatoes together.

To make the mayonnaise: In a blender or food processor, process the mustard, salt, pepper, and egg yolk until blended. With the machine running, add the oil in a thin stream and process until completely emulsified.

Gently mix the mayonnaise with the salad ingredients. Season with salt and pepper. Divide the salad among 4 plates, garnish with parsley, and serve.

Makes 4 servings

Poularde Marie-Louise

Chicken Marie-Louise

Serve this dish with steamed rice so that all the delicious sauce will be absorbed by the rice and not a drop wasted.

1 tablespoon butter

1 tablespoon oil

1 free-range roasting chicken, cut into serving pieces, or 6 chicken breasts

1 onion, chopped

2 pounds (1 kg) carrots, peeled and sliced

2 pounds (1 kg) tomatoes, quartered

1 fresh tarragon sprig

2 cups (16 fl oz/500 ml) dry white wine

1 tablespoon tomato paste

¾ cup (6 oz/185 g) crème fraîche (see Basics)

Salt and freshly ground black pepper to taste

In a large sauté pan or skillet over medium heat, melt the butter with the oil and sauté the chicken and onion until the chicken is golden brown, about 5 minutes on each side.

Transfer the chicken to a large, heavy pot. Add the carrots, tomatoes, tarragon, wine, and water to cover the chicken. Bring the water to a boil and skim off any foam that rises to the surface. Reduce heat to low and simmer for 30 minutes.

Using a slotted spoon, transfer the chicken pieces to a platter and cover loosely with aluminum foil to keep warm.

Transfer the cooking liquid and vegetables to a blender or food processor and purée. Return the sauce to the pot and stir in the tomato paste and crème fraîche. Add the chicken and simmer for 5 minutes.

Arrange a piece of chicken on each of 6 plates, spoon the sauce over, and serve.

Makes 6 servings

Crème Caramel

Caramel Custard

A smooth, comforting dessert.

5 tablespoons (2½ oz/75 g) granulated sugar

2 tablespoons water

2 cups (16 fl oz/500 ml) milk

1 vanilla bean, split lengthwise, or 1 teaspoon vanilla extract

1 cup (3½ oz/105 g) superfine sugar

3 eggs

Preheat the oven to 275°F (135°C). In a small, heavy saucepan, combine the sugar and water. Bring to a boil over high heat and cook until golden brown. Immediately remove from heat and pour the caramel into a 6-cup (48-fl oz/1.5-l) mold or divide among 6 individual ovenproof ramekins; tilt in all directions to coat partway up the sides; set aside.

In a small saucepan, combine the milk and vanilla bean, if using. Slowly bring to a boil over medium heat. Stir in the superfine sugar and remove the saucepan from heat. Set aside for 5 minutes to let the vanilla flavor infuse the milk. Remove the vanilla bean.

In a medium bowl, whisk the eggs until pale. Gradually whisk in the hot milk. Stir in the vanilla extract, if using.

Fill the caramelized mold or ramekins with the custard. Place the mold or ramekins in a baking pan and add hot water to reach halfway up the sides of the mold or ramekins. Bake in the preheated oven for 45 minutes, or until a knife inserted in the center of a custard comes out clean. Let cool completely before serving.

Makes 6 custards

CHEZ PAULINE

5, RUE VILLEDO, 75001 PARIS
MÉTRO PYRAMIDES

The perfect place for a business lunch or a special evening out, Chez Pauline is an elegant restaurant that has retained the spirit of its bistro roots. Located in the heart of Paris's financial district, Chez Pauline's doors have been open since the early 1900s. The current owner, Andre Génin, grew up in the bistro, which his parents bought in 1952. He took over in 1975 and still serves the old-fashioned Burgundian and Lyonnais menu created by his parents. To make sure that his young daughter (named Pauline after the bistro!) learns to love the cuisine he knows so well, Monsieur Génin has written *La Cuisine de Pauline*, a charming cookbook designed to help parents introduce their children to classic French cooking.

Chez Pauline's interior is chic and polished. Dark red banquettes, antique mirrored walls, thick white table linens, and huge pots of fresh flowers in the entryway create an atmosphere of quiet urbanity. Upstairs, two red-velveted dining rooms are plushly appointed with linens, crystal, and china.

Waiters at Chez Pauline, dressed in the traditional black and white, are friendly and quite knowledgeable about the superlative menu of seasonal bistro classics with some nouvelle touches. Specialties include fresh game in autumn and winter, beef Bourguignon, Skate with Crunchy Cabbage (page 155), and Rice Pudding (page 156). Meals at Chez Pauline start with an *amuse-bouche* (amusement for the taste buds) of *saucisson* (French salami) and finish with a delightful plate of farewell temptations that includes miniature pastries, delicate cookies, chocolates, and fresh fruit.

NEIGHBORHOOD WALK

Chez Pauline is within easy walking distance of several major tourist attractions, including the Louvre and the Pompidou Center. And yet, because it borders on the second arrondissement, Paris's banking center, the neighborhood around the bistro has its own particular character. In comparison to the crowded streets just a few blocks away, the atmosphere on rue Villedo seems almost sedate, suitable for those engaged in the serious business of finance.

Just east of Chez Pauline is a delightful example of how well Paris manages to combine the ancient and modern: the Palais-Royal. Built in the early seventeenth century for Cardinal Richelieu, the Palace is now home to France's Ministry of Culture and the Council of State. The townhouses that surround the Palace gardens were once home to both Colette and Jean Cocteau. Today, the houses are still used as dwelling places, while the ground-floor arcades are filled with shops, cafés, and restaurants. In 1986, artist Daniel Buren completed his controversial addition to the palace's central courtyard. Buren's 250 simple black and white columns of varying heights are a marked contrast to the historic buildings and gardens. Adjacent to the Palais-Royal complex is the Comédie Française, where classical French drama has been performed since 1790.

CHEZ PAULINE

Ris de Veau en Croûte, Façon Chez Pauline

Veal Sweetbreads in a Crust, Chez Pauline Style

Effiloché de Raie au Chou Croquant

Skate with Crunchy Cabbage

Riz au Lait Caramélisé

Caramelized Rice Pudding

Ris de Veau en Croûte, Façon Chez Pauline

Veal Sweetbreads in a Crust, Chez Pauline Style

This is the favorite dish of chef/owner André Génin's father, and it has been on Chez Pauline's menu since 1952. The preparations are time-consuming, but the delicate flavor and texture of the dish make it worthwhile.

1 pound (500 g) veal sweetbreads

1 onion, chopped

1 carrot, peeled and chopped

1 tablespoon minced fresh thyme

1 bay leaf

1½ tablespoons butter, melted

Salt and freshly ground black pepper to taste

1¼ cups (10 fl oz/310 ml) water

1 cup (8 fl oz/250 ml) dry white wine

1½ cups (12 fl oz/375 ml) heavy cream

Juice of ¼ lemon

8 ounces (250 g) puff pastry (see Basics)
   or thawed frozen puff pastry

¼ cup (2 fl oz/60 ml) white port

1 egg yolk beaten with 1 tablespoon water

16 white mushrooms, quartered

Place the sweetbreads in a bowl, cover with cold water, and soak for 1 hour.

Preheat the oven to 400°F (200°C). Bring a large saucepan of water to a boil, reduce heat to a simmer, add the sweetbreads, and cook for 8 minutes. Drain the sweetbreads and place them in a bowl of ice water for several minutes, or until they are fully cooled. Use a sharp knife to trim away all the membranes. Pat the sweetbreads dry with paper towels.

Spread the onion, carrot, thyme, and bay leaf in a flameproof casserole.

Arrange the sweetbreads on top, sprinkle with the butter, and season with salt and pepper. Pour in the water and wine. Bake in the preheated oven for 20 minutes, or until lightly browned. Turn the sweetbreads over and bake for another 20 minutes, or until lightly browned on the second side. Remove from the oven and transfer the sweetbreads to a plate. Leave the oven on.

Place the casserole over medium heat and bring the liquid to a boil. Stir in the cream, reduce heat, and simmer for 5 minutes; season with salt and pepper. Strain the sauce through a fine-meshed sieve. Pour in the port. Set aside and keep warm.

On a lightly floured board, roll the puff pastry out to a thickness of about ⅛ inch (3 mm). Cut into 4 equal-sized pieces. Cut the sweetbreads into 4 equal-sized pieces and wrap each in a square of puff pastry, pressing the edges closed to seal. Brush the pastry all over with the egg yolk mixture.

In a small bowl, whisk the egg yolk and water together. Brush the pastry with the egg yolk mixture and bake in the 400°F oven for 25 minutes, or until the pastry is golden brown.

In a medium sauté pan or skillet, bring the remaining ¼ cup (2 fl oz/60 ml) water and the lemon juice to a boil over medium heat. Add the mushrooms and cook for about 5 minutes, or until tender.

Spoon some of the sauce on each of 4 plates. Place a sweetbread in the center of each plate, spoon some of the mushrooms alongside, and serve immediately.

Makes 4 servings

Effiloché de Raie au Chou Croquant

Skate with Crunchy Cabbage

Skate is a fish with a delicate flavor somewhat similar to that of scallops. Choose a thick skate and have your fish seller fillet it.

1 small savoy or napa cabbage, cored and shredded

Salt and freshly ground black pepper to taste

2 tablespoons hazelnut oil or light olive oil

6 skate wing fillets (about 2 lb/1 kg total)

2 tomatoes, peeled, seeded, and diced (see Basics)

1 tablespoon white wine vinegar

2 teaspoons crushed hazelnuts

In a large pot of boiling water, blanch the shredded cabbage for 1 or 2 minutes, or until bright green. Drain and plunge into a bowl of cold water. Drain again and set the cabbage aside.

Season the fish lightly with salt and pepper. In a large sauté pan or skillet over medium heat, heat the oil and sauté the skate fillets for 4 minutes on each side, or until golden and cooked through. Using a slotted metal spatula, transfer to a plate.

In the same pan, sauté the cabbage just until heated through, 1 or 2 minutes. Add the tomatoes, vinegar, and hazelnuts and cook for 2 minutes.

Cut each skate fillet through on the diagonal several times, leaving the slices attached at the top. Arrange a portion of cabbage on each of 6 plates. Top each with a fillet and fan the slices open. Spoon some of the sauce over each fillet and serve immediately.

Makes 6 servings

Riz au Lait Caramélisé

Caramelized Rice Pudding

A very simple dish, but you've never had rice pudding this delicious. The distinctive French touch is caramelizing the baking dish as you would for a crème caramel. This pudding is especially good served warm.

Caramel

1 cup (8 oz/250 g) sugar

2 tablespoons water

6 cups (1.5 l) milk

²/₃ cup (5 oz/155 g) Arborio rice

¹/₃ cup sugar

1 vanilla bean, split lengthwise, or 1 teaspoon vanilla extract

¹/₂ cup (4 oz/125 g) unsalted butter, cut into bits

To make the caramel: In a small, heavy saucepan, combine the sugar and water. Bring to a boil over medium heat and cook for about 10 minutes, or until a light golden brown. Pour the caramel into a 6-cup (1.5 l) baking dish, tilting the dish in all directions to coat the bottom and partially up the sides.

In a large, heavy saucepan, combine the milk, rice, sugar, and vanilla bean, if using. Cook over low heat, stirring occasionally, for 1 hour and 30 minutes, or until the mixture thickens; do not boil. Stir in the vanilla extract, if using. Stir in the butter until it melts.

Pour the rice into the caramelized mold and set aside to cool slightly; do not refrigerate. Unmold the pudding onto a serving platter and serve it surrounded by its own caramel sauce, or serve scoops of the pudding on individual plates and surround with caramel sauce.

Makes 8 servings

LE PETIT MARGUERY

9, BOULEVARD DE PORT-ROYAL, 75013 PARIS

MÉTRO GOBELINS

Even though its size and bustle are reminiscent of a brasserie and many of its dishes are refined enough for a formal restaurant, Le Petit Marguery's relaxed atmosphere and generous servings of hearty food are unquestionably bistro. The rise and fall of happy French voices, the clink of glasses coming together for a toast, and the clatter of silverware against china create a party-like feel. Host Alain Cousin says his guests include chic, up-to-the-minute young people, networking businessmen, locals who save for months for a special feast, devoted regulars, and food-lovers from all over the world.

The three high-spirited Cousin brothers, Alain, Jacques, and Michel, purchased Le Petit Marguery in the early 1980s. After a careful refurbishing, their bistro's decor—vintage tile floors, hand-painted frescoes, and antique mirrors and sconces on rose-colored walls—creates a stylish setting for first-rate food prepared with great skill and imagination.

Chefs Jacques and Michel are especially known for their cassoulet, Petit Salé de Canard (page 164), fish specialties, and outstanding game dishes in the fall and winter. The bistro's extensive menu changes according to the time of year, but in each season dozens of their Grand Marnier soufflés are served for dessert every evening. As any of Le Petit Marguery's devoted regulars will tell you, this bistro is one of the best places in Paris to enjoy excellent French cuisine and a distinguished wine list in a fun and fashionable atmosphere.

NEIGHBORHOOD WALK

A few blocks south of Le Petit Marguery is the place d'Italie, where five major thoroughfares come together in one of the grand traffic circles typical of Paris. The wide shopping avenues of this neighbhorhood are intersected by many small residential streets, where academics, young families, and professionals make their homes. A walk from Le Petit Marguery towards the place d'Italie leads to the tapestry weaving factory created by Colbert to provide carpets and tapestries for Louis XIV—the Manufacture Nationale des Gobelins. The Gobelins factory still produces tapestries using ancient methods, and there are guided public tours of the workshops several days a week.

Not far from Le Petit Marguery, in the fifth arrondissement, is rue Mouffetard, a sloping cobblestoned street crowded with stores that sell everything from fresh pasta to inexpensive clothing. Mouffetard is worth a visit for its daily produce market, where you can see Parisians engaged in one of the activities they take most seriously—shopping for food. Young mothers carefully choose exactly the right piece of fish or bunch of parsley, couples spend long minutes discussing which cheeses to buy for the week, small children play in the spaces between fruit and vegetable stands, and in the background, the cries of produce vendors mingle with everyday street noises.

To the east of rue Mouffetard street is the Jardin des Plantes, the seventeenth-century site of the Royal medicinal herb garden, now a complex that includes Paris's museum of natural history and a pleasant botanical garden.

Le Petit Marguery

Saumon Mariné

Marinated Salmon

Petit Salé de Canard à la Poitevine

Brine-Cured Duck with Cabbage

Ile Flottante Caramélisée

Caramelized Floating Island

Saumon Mariné

Marinated Salmon

A spectacular first course: Thinly sliced salmon flavored with anise and green peppercorns and sprinkled with an herb vinaigrette. Begin preparations 3 days before you plan to serve this dish.

1 salmon fillet with skin, about 1½ pounds (750 g), boned

2 tablespoons coarse sea salt

1 tablespoon sugar

1 tablespoon crushed green peppercorns

1 tablespoon aniseed, ground, or Pernod

Vinaigrette

4 tablespoons (2 fl oz/60 ml) extra-virgin olive oil

1 tablespoon fresh lemon juice

Chopped fresh chives and parsley to taste

Using a sharp knife, slash the skin side of the salmon. In a small bowl, stir the salt, sugar, peppercorns, and aniseed, if using, together until thoroughly mixed. Place the salmon, skin-side down, in a glass pie plate and sprinkle the salt mixture over. Sprinkle with the Pernod, if using.

Cover the dish with plastic wrap. Wrap a piece of cardboard with aluminum foil and place on top of the fish. Top with a 2-pound (1-kg) weight to weigh the fish down evenly. Refrigerate for 3 days, occasionally spooning juices over the fish. After 1 day, remove the weight.

Using a very sharp knife, slice the fish thinly across the grain on a diagonal, cutting the flesh away from the skin.

To make the vinaigrette: In a small bowl, whisk all the ingredients together. Cover 4 plates with salmon slices and sprinkle with the vinaigrette.

Makes 4 servings

Petit Salé de Canard à la Poitevine

Brine-Cured Duck with Cabbage

Brining guarantees a moist, flavorful duck, and crisp, bright green savoy cabbage is a delicious counterpoint. Serve with boiled potatoes. Begin the preparations 5 days before you plan to serve this dish.

Brine

2 teaspoons chopped fresh thyme

2 garlic cloves, sliced

6 juniper berries, crushed

6 black peppercorns

2 whole cloves

4 cups (4 l) water

½ cup (4 oz/150 g) coarse sea salt

2 tablespoons sugar

6 whole duck legs (thigh and drumstick)

2 tablespoons butter

2 onions, chopped

1 leek, white part only, chopped

1 carrot, peeled and chopped

Cloves from 1 head garlic, minced

1 celery stalk, chopped

About 6 cups water and dry white wine, or as needed to cover duck

Salt and freshly ground black pepper to taste

Sauce

3 cups (24 fl oz/750 ml) reserved duck stock

¼ cup (2 fl oz/60 ml) heavy cream

2 egg yolks

Salt and freshly ground white pepper to taste

Cabbage

1 head savoy or napa cabbage, quartered, cored, and cut into strips

4 tablespoons (2 oz/60 g) unsalted butter

Salt and ground white pepper to taste

Five days before you plan to serve the duck, prepare the brine: In a small saucepan, bring the thyme, garlic, juniper berries, peppercorns, cloves, and 2 cups (16 fl oz/500 ml) of the water to a boil. Reduce heat, cover, and simmer for 10 minutes. Set aside to cool.

Meanwhile, in another medium saucepan combine the salt, sugar, and the remaining 2 cups (16 fl oz/500 ml) water. Cook over low heat, stirring until the salt dissolves. Set aside to cool.

In a large bowl, combine the cooled mixtures. Add the duck legs, cover, and refrigerate for 5 days.

The morning of the day you plan to serve the duck, drain the duck legs and discard the brine. Cover the duck with fresh cold water and set aside for 6 hours at room temperature.

In a large, heavy pot, melt the butter over medium heat and sauté the onions, leek, carrot, garlic, and celery until soft, about 10 minutes; do not let the onion brown. Add the duck legs and pour in water and an equal amount of white wine to cover the duck legs by 1 inch (2.5 cm). Add salt and pepper. Cover and simmer for 2 hours, or until the meat is very tender. Using a slotted spoon, transfer the duck legs to a plate and remove the skin. Return the duck pieces to the stock and keep warm over low heat.

To make the sauce: Transfer 3 cups (24 fl oz/750 ml) of the duck stock to a medium saucepan. Bring to a boil and cook to reduce the liquid by half, about 15 minutes. Reduce heat to low, stir in the cream and whisk in the egg yolks. Season with salt and pepper. Set aside and keep warm.

To cook the cabbage: In a large pot of salted boiling water, cook the cabbage until crisp-tender, about 5 minutes. Run under cold water and drain thoroughly. In a large sauté pan or skillet, melt the butter over medium heat and sauté the cabbage for about 2 minutes, tossing to coat with the butter. Season with salt and pepper.

To serve, arrange the cabbage on a warmed serving platter and the duck legs next to the cabbage. Spoon the sauce over the duck legs and cabbage and serve immediately.

Makes 6 servings

Ile Flottante Caramélisée

Caramelized Floating Island

Spoonfuls of baked meringue are coated with caramel and floated in a sea of custard in this classic French dessert. The meringue can be made several days ahead and refrigerated until serving time.

Caramel

⅔ cup (5 oz/155 g) granulated sugar

3 tablespoons (45 g) water

3 drops fresh lemon juice

1 cup (8 oz/250 g) granulated sugar

½ cup (2 oz/120 g) superfine sugar

8 eggs, separated

Pinch of salt

4 cups (1 l) milk

1 vanilla bean, split lengthwise, or 1 teaspoon vanilla extract

To make the caramel: In a small, heavy saucepan, combine the sugar, water, and lemon juice. Cover and cook over medium-high heat for 3 minutes, or until the bubbles are thick. Uncover the pan and continue boiling until the mixture turns golden brown. Immediately remove from heat, swirling the pan as the caramel continues to color. Quickly pour into an 8-cup baking dish, tilting the mold in all directions to coat it partway up the sides. Set aside to cool.

Preheat the oven to 325°F (165°C). In a small bowl, mix the granulated sugar with ¼ cup (2 oz/60 g) of the superfine sugar.

In a large bowl, beat the egg whites with the salt until soft peaks form. Gradually beat in the sugar mixture until stiff, glossy peaks form. Pour into the caramelized mold.

Place the mold in a larger baking dish and fill the dish with hot water to come halfway up the sides of the mold. Bake in the preheated oven for 30 to 40 minutes minutes, or until a knife inserted in the center comes out clean. Let cool and refrigerate until serving time.

In a medium saucepan, combine the milk and vanilla bean, if using, and slowly bring to a boil over medium-low heat. Immediately remove from heat, cover, and let sit for 10 minutes so the vanilla flavor infuses the milk. Remove the vanilla bean. If not using the vanilla bean, stir the vanilla extract into the hot milk.

In a medium bowl, beat the egg yolks with the remaining ¼ cup (2 oz/60 g) superfine sugar for 1 minute, or until pale. Very gradually whisk the hot milk into the egg mixture. Pour into a saucepan and stir constantly over low heat for about 10 minutes, or until the custard thickens enough to coat the back of the spoon. Do not let the mixture boil, or the eggs will curdle. Remove from heat and let cool.

To serve: Pour the crème anglaise into 6 serving bowls and add a large spoonful of the cooled egg whites to each. Spoon the caramel sauce over and serve immediately.

Makes 8 servings

AU PIED DE FOUET

45, RUE DE BABYLONE, 75007 PARIS

MÉTRO VANEAU OR ST-FRANÇOIS-XAVIER

Au Pied de Fouet offers simple home-style cooking to a local clientele of writers, architects, and government workers, many of whom dine at the tiny bistro on a regular basis. The evening we sat chatting with Monsieur Chich, the bistro's proprietor, he was checking the mirror behind us for the entrance of regulars, for whom he rose and offered a friendly greeting and often a kiss on both cheeks.

In the late 1700s, this space was a bar where servants from a nearby grand residence stopped for a drink and perhaps a *casse-croûte* (snack) after work. In addition, riders traveling from Versaille came here to replenish themselves and to water their horses. The name Au Pied de Fouet dates from those days: A *pied de fouet* is a horsewhip holder. Fittingly, the dining room is hung with harnesses, wagon wheels, and other equestrian paraphernalia.

Au Pied de Fouet is quite well known—and with only five tables and a first-rate menu of bistro classics at bargain prices, it fills up fast. There are no reservations, so you'll probably spend a few minutes enjoying an aperitif at the zinc bar while you wait for a table.

The bistro is furnished with an authentic *meuble à serviette*, a many-drawered napkin cabinet, which is still used to hold the napkins of some regulars. According to Monsieur Chich, it takes more than eating at his establishment regularly to warrant your own personal drawer. "It's a question of feeling," he says—whether someone makes an effort to move beyond the realm of customer into that of friendship. The hundreds of postcards that hang from the bistro's ceiling are a testament to the many satisfied diners who consider themselves friends of Au Pied de Fouet.

NEIGHBORHOOD WALK

The streets in Au Pied de Fouet's seventh-arrondissement neighborhood are lined with foreign embassies and French ministries, including the Hôtel de Matignon, where the French prime minister makes his home. In keeping with the neighborhood's grand atmosphere is Les Invalides, a hospital founded by Louis XIV for wounded and ill soldiers. Besides the hospital, the complex includes the splendid gold-domed Hôtel des Invalides and a tree-lined esplanade. The French military administration is headquartered here, and a military museum is open for visitors.

Right next door to Invalides is the Musée Rodin. Housed in the Hôtel Biron, the museum is dedicated to the works of French artist and sculptor Auguste Rodin. In the early 1900s, the Biron mansion was divided into studios for artists and writers, including Rodin and poet Rainer Maria Rilke. Eventually, Rodin moved into the mansion, where he lived until his death.

The Musée d'Orsay is a very pleasant fifteen- or twenty-minute walk from Au Pied de Fouet. The art museum was originally a train station, built in the late 1800s to serve southwestern France. Orsay houses a major collection of late nineteenth- and early twentieth-century art, including many famous Impressionist works. The museum, which still retains the open, airy feel of a belle-époque train station, is extremely popular with Parisians, as well as art-lovers from all over the world.

AU PIED DE FOUET

Courgettes et Tomates à l'Aixoise
Provençal Vegetable Terrine

Jambonette de Volaille et Sa Crème de Ciboulette
Chicken with Chive Cream Sauce

Gâteau au Chocolat
Chocolate Cake

Courgettes et Tomates à l'Aixoise

Provençal Vegetable Terrine

A festive layered vegetable terrine that highlights some of the best flavors of Provence.

2 tablespoons olive oil, plus more for drizzling

1 onion, thinly sliced

1 red bell pepper, seeded, deribbed, and diced

3 zucchini, thinly sliced

3 tomatoes, thinly sliced

6 ounces (185 g) white mushrooms, thinly sliced

3 garlic cloves, minced

Salt and freshly ground black pepper to taste

3 bay leaves

Herbes de Provence or minced fresh thyme for sprinkling

Preheat the oven to 300°F (150°C). Lightly coat a 9-by-5-inch (23-by-13-cm) terrine or loaf pan with olive oil.

In a medium sauté pan or skillet over medium heat, heat the 2 tablespoons olive oil and sauté the onion for 3 minutes, or until translucent. Add the bell pepper and sauté for 5 minutes.

Transfer the red pepper mixture to the terrine or loaf pan and spread to make an even layer. Top with a layer of half of the zucchini, a layer of half of the tomato, and a layer of all the mushrooms. Drizzle with olive oil and sprinkle with the garlic, salt, and pepper.

For the top layer, alternate the remaining tomato and zucchini slices. Drizzle with olive oil and tuck the bay leaves among the tomato and zucchini slices. Sprinkle with salt and pepper to taste and the herb(s). Cover with aluminum foil and bake in the preheated oven for 2 hours, or until the vegetables are very soft and tender. Remove from the oven and let cool to room temperature before serving.

Makes 6 to 8 servings

Jambonette de Volaille et sa Crème Ciboulette

Chicken with Chive Cream Sauce

This dish is made with whole chicken legs that are boned so that they resemble little hams. You can use boneless chicken breasts as a substitute. Serve this delicious spring-green dish with steamed new potatoes and a Beaujolais or Pinot Noir.

2 pounds (1 kg) tiny new red potatoes (12 to 16 potatoes)

1 pound (500 g) boned whole chicken legs
  (thighs and drumsticks), or 4 boneless chicken breasts

Salt and freshly ground black pepper to taste

Flour for dredging, plus3 tablespoons flour

2 tablespoons unsalted butter, plus 2 tablespoons butter
  at room temperature

1/2 cup (2 oz/60 g) coarsely chopped onion

2 cups (16 fl oz/500 ml) chicken stock (see Basics)
  or canned low-salt chicken broth

3/4 cup (30 cl) crème fraîche (see Basics)

2 bunches fresh chives, coarsely chopped

In a covered steamer, steam the potatoes over boiling water for 20 minutes, or until tender when pierced with a knife.

Meanwhile, sprinkle the chicken pieces with salt and pepper. Just before sautéing, dredge the chicken in flour and shake off the excess.

In a large sauté pan or skillet, melt the 2 tablespoons butter over medium heat and sauté the chicken for 2 minutes on each side, or until golden. Reduce heat to low, stir in the onion, cover, and cook for 15 minutes, turning the chicken once. Transfer the chicken pieces to a plate; set aside and keep warm.

To make the sauce: In the same pan over medium heat, stir the stock or broth to scrape up the browned bits from the bottom of the pan. Raise heat to high and cook to reduce the liquid by a third. Reduce heat to medium

low, stir in the crème fraîche, and slowly bring to a boil.

Knead the 2 tablespoons soft butter and 3 tablespoons flour together to make a paste. Whisk the paste into the sauce until smooth. Season with salt and pepper to taste. Simmer for 5 minutes, whisking often, until smooth and thick.

In a blender or food processor, purée the chives. Add the sauce and process until smooth.

To serve, place a chicken piece on each of 4 plates and spoon over some of the chive sauce. Serve immediately, with steamed potatoes on the side.

Make 4 servings

Gâteau au Chocolat

Chocolate Cake

7 ounces (220 g) bittersweet chocolate, chopped

6 eggs, separated

1/3 cup (3 oz/90 g) sugar

1/3 cup (2 oz/60 g) unbleached all-purpose flour

1 cup (3.5 oz/90 g) ground blanched almonds

1/4 teaspoon salt

1/3 cup vegetable oil

2 teaspoons baking powder

1 teaspoon baking soda

8 ounces (125 g) sweet chocolate, chopped

Preheat the oven to 300°F (150°C). Butter the bottom of a 9-inch (23 cm) springform pan.

In a double boiler over barely simmering water, melt the bittersweet chocolate; remove from heat and set aside. In a large bowl, beat the egg whites until stiff, glossy peaks form.

In a medium bowl, beat the sugar and eggs yolks together until thick and pale. Stir in the flour, ground almonds, salt, oil, baking powder, and baking soda and beat until thoroughly blended. Pour in the melted chocolate and stir until mixed. Stir in one fourth of the egg whites. Gently fold in the remaining whites until thoroughly blended.

Pour the batter into the prepared pan and bake in the preheated oven for 40 to 45 minutes, or until a knife inserted in the center comes out clean. Remove from the oven and let cool completely.

In a double boiler over barely simmering water, melt the sweet chocolate. Remove from heat and let cool until firm enough to spread. Spoon on top of the cake and spread over the top and sides to make a mirrorlike glaze.

Makes one 9-inch (24-cm) cake; serves 8

CRÉMERIE RESTAURANT POLIDOR

41, RUE MONSIEUR-LE-PRINCE, 75006 PARIS
MÉTRO ODÉON, LUXEMBOURG, OR CLUNY

Crémerie Restaurant Polidor started out in the second half of the nineteenth century as a store that sold milk, eggs, and cheeses to local matrons and their servants. In 1890, the crémerie was sold to Monsieur Froissard, who turned it into a bistro. Froissard's place soon became popular among locals, including the poet Rimbaud, who was a neighbor on rue Monsieur-le-Prince.

By the 1950s, a group of leading French writers, artists, and philosophers had formed a social group, whimsically named the "College of Pataphysics" (the science of imaginary solutions), with Polidor as their headquarters. Famous foreigners, such as James Joyce, Ernest Hemingway, and Max Ernst, were also regulars at Polidor's tables. These days, students, professors, and international tourists enjoy the bistro's extensive, inexpensive menu.

Proprietor André Maillet oversees every aspect of Polidor's operations. Like most bistro owners, he is devoted to making sure his establishment continues to live up to its illustrious history. In true bistro fashion, his regulars still receive kisses on both cheeks and their preferred aperitif as soon as they approach the bistro's zinc bar. Polidor's menu offers home-style dishes and an assortment of pastries, which are baked fresh daily in an underground bakery next door. The bistro's vintage tiled floors, numbered napkin drawers, painted murals, and oilcloth-covered tables all contribute to an antiquated and charming atmosphere in which to enjoy generous portions of bistro cuisine in the Latin Quarter.

NEIGHBORHOOD WALK

A few blocks from Polidor is boulevard St-Michel, the center of the Latin Quarter. Although there are Roman ruins nearby, the name Quartier Latin dates back only to the twelfth century. At that time, young people came from all over the world to study at a theological college in this Left Bank neighborhood, and Latin was often their only common language. That first college evolved into today's Sorbonne, still the heart of Paris's university system, and the reason for all the chic yet exhausted-looking students you see on boulevard St-Michel. An oasis of calm on the otherwise busy street is the Musée National du Moyen Age. This museum is devoted to the arts of the Middle Ages and is housed in a fifteenth-century *hôtel* (or mansion) that was built on the site of second-century Roman baths. The remains of the baths still exist and can be seen while visiting the museum, along with a marvelous collection of medieval tapestries, manuscripts, and music.

Near Polidor on rue Monsieur-le-Prince, visitors will find a fascinating mix of bistros, residences, bookshops, and small cluttered stores that sell everything from artists' mannequins to supplies for medical students.

POLIDOR

Crème de Lentilles Blondes

Yellow Lentil Soup

Filet d'Agneau aux Soissons
et Aumônières de Légumes

Lamb with White Beans and Vegetable Purses

Tarte Tatin

Upside-Down Apple Tart

Mousse au Chocolat

Chocolate Mousse

Crème de Lentilles Blondes

Yellow Lentil Soup

Although proprietor André Maillet suggests garnishing each bowl of soup with a truffle slice or two, this easy-to-make soup may be made without either truffles or foie gras.

⅓ cup (3 oz/90 g) butter

1 onion, minced

1 carrot, peeled and chopped

One 2-ounce (50 g) piece slab bacon or smoked ham

1 cup (7 oz/220 g) dried yellow lentils

Bouquet garni; 1 parsley sprig, 1 thyme sprig, and 1 bay leaf, tied in a cheesecloth square

Salt and freshly ground black pepper to taste

3½ ounces (105 g) foie gras (see Resources), chopped (optional)

2 cups (16 fl oz/500 ml) heavy cream or half-and-half

1 truffle, thinly sliced, for garnish (optional)

In a large saucepan, melt the butter over medium heat and sauté the onion, carrot, and ham for 5 minutes, or until the onions are soft. Add the lentils, bouquet garni, and water to cover by 2 inches (5 cm). Season with salt and pepper and cook over low heat for about 30 minutes, stirring occasionally. Remove from heat and remove the bouquet garni and bacon or ham with a slotted spoon. Swirl in the foie gras, if using, until melted.

Transfer the soup to a blender or food processor and purée, or use a potato masher or fork to mash the soup. Pour the soup back into the saucepan, stir in the cream, and simmer over medium heat for 5 minutes. Taste and adjust the seasoning.

Ladle the soup into shallow soup bowls, garnish with a few truffle slices, if desired, and serve immediately.

Makes 6 to 8 servings

Filet d'Agneau aux Soissons et Aumônières de Légumes

Lamb with White Beans and Vegetable Purses

Try a glass of Côtes-du-Rhône or Merlot with this hearty dish.

2½ cups (500 g) dried navy beans or Great Northern beans

4 tablespoons olive oil

1 saddle of lamb (2 loins), boned

3 carrots, peeled and chopped

3 onions, chopped

2 garlic cloves, crushed

1 fresh rosemary sprig

3 tomatoes, peeled, seeded, and neatly diced (see Basics)

2 tablespoons peanut oil

7 ounces (220 g) mushrooms, finely chopped

5 fresh basil leaves

5 green olives, pitted and chopped

¾ cup (6 fl oz/180 ml) heavy cream

½ cup (4 oz/125 g) butter

3 cups (3 oz/90 g) packed spinach leaves, blanched for 2 minutes and drained

Salt and freshly ground black pepper to taste

8 Swiss chard leaves, blanched for 4 minutes and drained

Pick over and rinse the beans. Soak overnight in cold water to cover by 2 inches (5 cm); drain. Alternatively, place the beans in a large saucepan with cold water to cover by 2 inches (5 cm). Bring to a boil, cook for 2 minutes, then turn off heat and let soak for 1 hour; drain.

In a Dutch oven or flameproof casserole over high heat, heat 2 tablespoons of the olive oil and brown the lamb bone on all sides. Add the carrots,

onions, garlic, and rosemary. Add water to cover and simmer for 3 to 4 hours, skimming off any foam that rises to the surface.

Put the beans in a large pot and add water to cover by 2 inches (5 cm); bring to a boil. Reduce heat to low and simmer, stirring frequently, until the beans are tender, about 1 hour. Stir in half of the tomatoes and the lamb stock.

In a medium sauté pan or skillet over medium-high heat, heat the peanut oil and sauté the mushrooms until they are lightly browned and all the water has evaporated. Stir in the remaining tomatoes, the basil, olives, cream, and butter. Cook to reduce by one third. Stir in the spinach leaves, salt, and pepper; set aside.

Lay the chard leaves out flat on a work surface and place equal amounts of the mushroom mixture in the center of each. Draw up the sides of the chard leaves and twist to make 8 pouches.

In a large sauté pan or skillet over medium-high heat, heat the remaining 2 tablespoons olive oil and brown the lamb loins for 4 minutes on each side for medium rare. Slice the lamb thinly and divide the meat, beans, and vegetable purses among 8 dinner plates; serve immediately.

Makes 8 servings

Tarte Tatin

Upside-Down Apple Tart

Made famous by the two Tatin sisters, who ran a restaurant in the village of Lamotte-Beuvron early in the 1900s, this delicious caramelized upside-down apple tart is served in most bistros.

Pastry

1½ cups (7½ oz/235 g) all-purpose flour

½ cup (4 oz/125 g) butter, cut into small pieces

¼ cup (2 oz/60 g) sugar

2 eggs

Filling

5 to 6 Golden Delicious or Granny Smith apples
    (about 2 lb/1 kg), peeled, cored, and quartered

2 cups (16 oz/500 g) sugar

¾ cup (6 fl oz/185 ml) water

⅔ cup (5 oz/150 g) butter

1 teaspoon vanilla extract

Crème fraîche (see Basics), whipped cream,
    or vanilla ice cream for serving

To make the pastry: In a blender or food processor, add all the ingredients and process until the dough begins to form a ball, about 20 seconds. Alternatively, put all the ingredients in a medium bowl and use a fork to combine. Work with your fingertips until the mixture can be formed into a ball. On a lightly floured board, knead the dough a few times until smooth. Flatten the dough into a disk, cover with plastic wrap, and refrigerate for at least 45 minutes, or up to 2 hours.

Preheat the oven to 400°F (200°C). To make the filling: In a medium, heavy saucepan over high heat, combine the sugar and water. Bring to a boil and cook until a deep golden brown. Remove from heat and stir in the butter and vanilla. Quickly pour the caramel into a heavy ovenproof 9-inch

(23-cm) skillet; let cool. Cut the apple quarters in half lengthwise. Arrange the apples in a neat, tight spiral over the caramel; top with all the remaining apple slices to form a second layer. The apples will sink down when they cook so be generous. Bake in the preheated oven for 45 minutes.

On a lightly floured surface, roll the dough out into a 10-inch (25-cm) circle. Lay the pastry over the apples, tucking the dough down into the dish around the edges. Cut 4 steam vents in the center of the dough and bake for about 25 minutes, or until the pastry is golden brown. Carefully remove from the oven and let cool. Place a serving platter on top of the baking dish and invert to unmold the tart, giving the bottom a firm whack to release the apples on the bottom. Serve warm or at room temperature, with crème fraîche, whipped cream, or vanilla ice cream.

Makes one 10-inch (25-cm) tart; serves 8 to 10

Mousse au Chocolat

Chocolate Mousse

A classic bistro dessert for those who love chocolate—enjoy!

7 ounces (220 g) bittersweet chocolate, chopped

²/₃ cup (5 oz/155 g) unsalted butter, cut into small pieces

1 teaspoon powdered espresso

8 eggs, separated

²/₃ cup (5 oz/155 g) sugar

¾ cup (6 fl oz/180 ml) heavy cream

In a double boiler over barely simmering water, melt the chocolate. Remove from heat and stir in the butter and espresso until blended.

In a medium bowl, whisk the egg yolks and ⅓ cup (3 oz/90g) of the sugar together until thick and pale. Beat in the chocolate mixture. Stir in the cream.

In a large bowl, beat the egg whites until soft peaks form. Gradually beat in the remaining ⅓ cup (3 oz/90 g) sugar until stiff, glossy peaks form. Stir one fourth of the egg whites into the chocolate mixture. Gently fold the egg whites into the chocolate mixture until thoroughly blended.

Pour into 10 individual serving bowls or 1 large serving bowl, cover with plastic wrap, and refrigerate for at least 6 hours or preferably overnight.

Makes 10 servings

LA POULE AU POT

9, RUE VAUVILLIERS, 75001 PARIS
MÉTRO LOUVRE OR LES HALLES

La Poule au Pot is one of Paris's celebrated *bistros de nuit*—bistros of the night. Open from 7 pm to 6 am every night, La Poule is especially popular among entertainers visiting Paris. Brass plaques on the wall above the red moleskin banquettes in the main dining room bear the names of some of the bistro's celebrated visitors—from Frank Sinatra and Sting, to actors Dustin Hoffman and Marcello Mastrionni, to model Kate Moss and architect M. Pei—the list goes on and on. If you ask proprietor Paul Racat about La Poule au Pot's *livre d'or*, he'll show you a guest book filled with signatures, *bon mots*, and doodles of famous luminaries.

Paul Racat has been the beaming, genial presence behind La Poule au Pot for almost twenty-five years. Founded in 1935 by Suzanne Peniquet, the bistro survived World War II largely intact. Legend has it that she saved the bistro's handsome curved bar and its gleaming copper counter from the Germans, who confiscated most of the metal fixtures in the city. Today the bistro's vintage radio, columns covered with gold-glass mosaic tiles, and glittering Art Deco light fixtures still evoke the 1930s.

The cuisine at Poule au Pot is as stylish as the interior. Dishes like Salade Poule au Pot (spinach salad with sautéed chicken livers) page 195, the bistro's celebrated Gratinée des Halles, (French onion soup) page 196, and the quintessential Poule au Pot Garnié (steaming broth, vegetables, and stewed chicken in a large soup tureen) page 198 are served by friendly waiters dressed in the traditional black and white. If you can wait until after midnight for your dinner, you'll be rewarded with extremely generous portions of bistro classics and a chance to see the bright young things of Paris in their element.

NEIGHBORHOOD WALK

La Poule au Pot is situated in a neighborhood that is particularly important to bistro history—Les Halles. When most of the Parisian bistros in this book first opened, their owners started every day with an early-morning visit to the Marché aux Halles, the central food market of Paris.

In the early twelfth century, Paris's principal market was moved from the Ile de la Cité (an island in the Seine and the first inhabited part of Paris) to a neighborhood north of the Seine known as Beaubourg. At first, the *marché* was for craftspeople and tradesmen, as well as sellers of foodstuffs. Within a few hundred years, the population of Paris had grown enough to support an entire market devoted to comestibles. In the mid-nineteenth century, ten giant halls were built on the site, creating the prototype for Europe's covered markets. Les Halles continued to provide sustenance for France's capital until 1969. Today, Parisian restaurants stock their larders at Rungis, the wholesale food market located just south of Paris near the Orly airport.

Les Halles itself has become a giant subterranean shopping complex, with terraces and gardens above ground. Around the gardens, a few old-style bistros remain as a reminder of the years when restaurant owners, butchers, and produce sellers met at all hours of day and night for hearty classics like *gratinée des Halles*, or as we know it, French Onion Soup (page 196).

LA POULE AU POT

Salade Poule au Pot

Spinach Salad with Sautéed Chicken Livers

Gratinée des Halles

French Onion Soup

Poule au Pot Garnie

Poached Stuffed Chicken with Vegetables

Soufflés Glacés au Framboise

Frozen Raspberry Soufflés

Soufflés Glacés au Grand Marnier

Frozen Grand Marnier Soufflés

Salade Poule au Pot

Spinach Salad with Sautéed Chicken Livers

1 pound (500 g) spinach, stemmed, washed, dried, and chopped into large pieces

2 tablespoons peanut oil

8 ounces (125 g) chicken livers, quartered

1 onion

1/4 teaspoon ground white pepper

3 tablespoons dry white wine

3 tablespoons red wine vinegar

3 tablespoons reduced beef or veal stock (see Basics) or canned beef broth

Put the spinach in a salad bowl and set aside. In a large sauté pan or skillet over medium-high heat, heat the oil and sauté the chicken livers, onion, and pepper until the livers are browned, about 2 minutes. Stir in the wine, then the vinegar, and finally the stock or broth, mixing to coat the livers well. Lower the heat to medium low and simmer for 3 minutes, stirring occasionally.

Remove the pan from heat and spoon the hot livers and sauce over the spinach. Bring to the table, toss, and serve immediately on 4 individual salad plates.

Makes 4 servings

Gratinée des Halles

French Onion Soup

A large bowl of this hearty soup becomes a meal in itself when served with a green salad and some fresh fruit or other dessert. The soup is even more flavorful when prepared a day in advance.

¼ cup (2 fl oz/60 ml) vegetable oil

5 large yellow onions (about 2½ pounds/1.25 g), thinly sliced

2 cups (16 fl oz/500 ml) dry white wine

8 cups (2 l) Hearty Chicken and Beef stock (see Basics) or canned low-salt chicken broth

Salt and freshly ground black pepper to taste

Eight ¾-inch-thick (2-cm) slices day-old French bread

3 cups (12 oz/375 g) shredded Gruyère or Swiss cheese

In a large, heavy pot casserole over high heat, heat the oil until almost smoking. Add the onions and reduce heat to medium. Cook the onions for about 30 minutes, or until they are soft and an even deep golden brown; stir frequently with a wooden spoon and scrape up all the browned bits from the bottom of the pan.

Pour in the wine, raise heat to high, and boil until the soup is reduced by two thirds. Stir in the stock or broth and bring to a boil. Reduce heat to low and simmer for 20 minutes. Season with salt and pepper. (At this point, you can refrigerate the soup, covered, for up to 3 days; bring to a simmer before continuing.)

Preheat the broiler. Place 8 deep ovenproof soup bowls or crocks on a baking sheet. Ladle the soup into the bowls, add a slice of the bread to each bowl, and sprinkle the shredded cheese on top. Broil for 3 to 4 minutes, or until the cheese is golden and bubbling. Serve immediately.

Makes 6 servings

Poule au Pot Garnie

Poached Stuffed Chicken with Vegetables

King Henri IV decreed that every French family should have a chicken in the pot each Sunday, and this dish is still a wonderful way to gather our families close at the end of a weekend.

One 3½- to 4-pound (1.75- to 2-kg) chicken

4 ounces (125 g) lean ground pork

4 ounces (125 g) ground veal

⅓ cup (2 oz/60 g) minced onion, plus 1 large onion, studded with 3 whole cloves

1 tablespoon minced fresh parsley

1 egg yolk

½ teaspoon salt

¼ teaspoon freshly ground black pepper

6 carrots, peeled and cut into ½-inch (12-mm) slices

4 leeks, white parts only

4 turnips, cut into ½-inch (12-mm) dice

1 large onion, studded with 3 whole cloves

2 celery stalks, cut into 2-inch (5-cm) pieces

Bouquet garni: 1 thyme sprig, 1 parsley sprig, and 1 bay leaf, tied in a cheesecloth square

8 small potatoes, peeled

Clean the chicken, removing all excess fat. Combine the pork, veal, minced onion, parsley, egg yolk, salt, and pepper in a bowl. Fill the body cavity of the chicken with the pork mixture and truss the chicken with kitchen string. Place the chicken in a large pot. Add all the remaining ingredients except the potatoes. Add cold water to cover the chicken and bring to a boil. Reduce heat to low, cover, and simmer for 2 hours.

Add the potatoes and cook for 25 minutes, or until the potatoes are tender when pierced with a knife. Taste and adjust the seasoning. Remove the chicken and vegetables from the stock and keep warm. Spoon off as much fat as possible from the broth. Slice the stuffing and breast and cut the chicken into serving pieces: wings, legs, thighs.

Serve from a large soup tureen, filling each soup bowl with chicken, a slice of stuffing, some vegetables, and broth. Or, serve as two courses, the broth first, followed by the chicken and sliced stuffing on a platter surrounded by the vegetables, all moistened with broth. Serve with sea salt, gherkins, and mustard.

Makes 8 servings

Note: Any remaining broth makes a great soup or sauce base.

Soufflés Glacés au Framboise

Frozen Raspberry Soufflés

A light and refreshing dessert.

2 cups (8 oz/250 g) fresh raspberries

1½ tablespoons plus ½ cup (4 oz/125 g) sugar

½ teaspoon plus 1½ tablespoons water

3 egg whites

½ cup (4 oz/125 g) crème fraîche (see Basics)

½ pint (8 oz/250 g) raspberry sorbet or sherbet

4 fresh mint leaves for garnish

Line four 4-inch (10-cm) ramekins or bowls with plastic wrap, allowing the edges of the plastic to hang over the sides.

In a medium saucepan, combine the raspberries, the 1½ tablespoons sugar, and the ½ teaspoon water; bring to a boil, stirring occasionally. Remove from heat and let cool. Strain through a fine-meshed sieve to remove the seeds. You should have about ½ cup (4 fl oz/125 ml) purée. Set aside.

In a small, heavy saucepan, combine the remaining ½ cup (4 oz/125 g) sugar and the 1½ tablespoons water. Cook over medium-high heat until the syrup forms a ribbon (238°F/112°C on a candy thermometer).

Using an electric mixer, beat the egg whites in a large bowl until soft peaks form. While beating at medium speed, very gradually pour the sugar syrup down the side of the bowl. Continue to beat the meringue until stiff, glossy peaks form. Fold ¼ cup (2 fl oz/60 ml) of the raspberry purée into the meringue. In a deep bowl, whip the crème fraîche until soft peaks form. Fold the crème fraîche into the meringue. Divide half the meringue among the prepared ramekins or bowls. Add a scoop of raspberry sorbet and cover completely with the remaining meringue. Cover each ramekin with plastic wrap and freeze for at least 2 hours.

To serve, pour some of the remaining raspberry purée onto each of 4 chilled serving dishes. Carefully invert the soufflés onto the plates and remove the plastic wrap. Garnish each soufflé with a mint leaf and serve immediately.

Makes four 4-inch (10-cm) soufflés

LA POULE AU POT

Soufflés Glacés au Grand Marnier

Frozen Grand Marnier Soufflés

8 tablespoons (4 oz/125 g) sugar

7 tablespoons (3½ fl oz/95 ml) water

5 large eggs, separated

1½ cups (12 oz/375 g) crème fraîche (see Basics)

½ cup (4 fl oz/125 ml) Grand Marnier

8 ladyfingers (see Basics)

Orange Sauce

½ cup (5 oz/155 g) orange marmalade

2 tablespoons orange juice

2 tablespoons Grand Marnier

In a small, heavy saucepan, boil 4 tablespoons (2 oz/60 g) of the sugar and 4 tablespoons (2 fl oz/60 ml) of the water until syrupy.

In a double boiler over barely simmering water, whisk the egg yolks until pale. Gradually whisk in the hot syrup, cooking for 2 minutes. Be careful not to let the yolk mixture boil, as it will curdle.

Put the remaining sugar and water in a small, heavy saucepan. Cook over medium heat until the syrup forms a ribbon (238°F/112°C on a candy thermometer). In a large bowl, beat the egg whites until soft peaks form. Gradually pour the sugar syrup down the side of the bowl and continue beating until stiff, glossy peaks form.

In a deep bowl, beat the crème fraîche until soft peaks form. Fold in ¼ cup (2 fl oz/60 ml) of the Grand Marnier. Fold the yolk mixture into the crème fraîche, then fold into the meringue.

Line 8 individual soufflé dishes with plastic wrap, letting the edges hang over the sides. Spoon half of the meringue mixture into each dish. Brush the ladyfingers with the remaining Grand Marnier. Place 2 ladyfingers, cut to fit on top of each meringue, and fill the dishes with the remaining meringue. Cover with plastic wrap and freeze for at least 2 hours.

To make the orange sauce: In a small saucepan, melt the marmalade over low heat. Stir in the orange juice and Grand Marnier.

To serve, invert the soufflé dishes onto 8 chilled plates and spoon the orange sauce over.

Makes 8 individual soufflés

CHEZ TOUTOUNE

This cozy bistro reflects the Provençal heritage of its owner, Colette Dejean. Although Madame Dejean has lived in Paris all her life, both her parents are from the South of France, and everything at her bistro, from decor to cuisine, is Provençal. As soon as you enter Chez Toutoune, the flowered curtains, lush green plants, and waiters in soft blue-green shirts seem to transport you away from Paris to a sunnier climate. Even the dining room's table linens and pottery are specially made in the South of France.

Meals begin with tapenade (olive paste) on rounds of country bread, and if it strikes your fancy, Pastis, an anise-flavored aperitif made in Provence. The traditional start to the bistro's prix fixe menu is a tureen of the soup of the day, which is followed by a seasonal appetizer and a main dish such as Estouffade de Joue de Boeuf, Macaroni au Parmesan (Braised Beef Cheeks with Parmesan Macaroni), page 208. For dessert, Toutoune's orange-flavored crème brûlée is especially delightful. Today, this dessert's crisp sugar topping is melted by using a blowtorch or preheated broiler; however, Colette Dejean says that years ago hot irons were held near the sugar to caramelize the sugar.

Madame Dejean opened Chez Toutoune in 1979 and has been delighting diners in the fifth arrondissement every since. Toutoune is actually Madame Dejean's own childhood nickname—it's a friendly term of endearment derived from Colette—and in fact, some regulars at her thirteen tables feel enough at home to call her by this familiar name.

NEIGHBORHOOD WALK

On Tuesdays, Thursdays, and Saturdays, the stairs from métro station Maubert-Mutualité lead to the Carmes marché, one of many produce markets where Parisians do their daily or weekly shopping. The market offers towers of fresh vegetables, buckets of beautiful flowers, baskets of mussels and scallops, cheeses, breads—enough to make you want to give up on the idea of eating out and shop for a picnic at home!

One block away from Chez Toutoune is the Quai de la Tournelle, an embankment along the Seine facing Ile St-Louis and Ile de la Cité. These two islands, almost the geographical center of Paris, are the oldest inhabited parts of the city. Several major sight-seeing destinations are located on Ile de la Cité, including Notre Dame Cathedral and the jewel-like Ste-Chapelle, which was built as a royal chapel for Louis IX in 1248. The beautiful Ile St-Louis is mostly residential, but ice cream-lovers should be sure to stop at Berthillon on the island's main street for the best ice cream in the city. The views from the bridges between the quai and the islands are among the most romantic in Paris. The cobblestone streets, Notre Dame's flying buttresses, the sky over the glorious Seine, and the formal rows of seventeenth-century buildings on the Ile St-Louis create a classically Parisian scene.

CHEZ TOUTOUNE

Aïgo Bouido

Provençal Garlic Soup

Estouffade de Joue de Boeuf, Macaroni au Parmesan

Braised Beef Cheeks with Parmesan Macaroni

Crème Brûlée à la Fleur d'Oranges

Orange-Flavored Burned Cream

Aïgo Bouido

Provençal Garlic Soup

An absolutely delicious Mediterranean soup.

¼ cup (2 fl oz/60 ml) olive oil

3 leeks, white parts only, thinly sliced

4 onions, minced

1 large head garlic, unpeeled cloves separated and smashed

2 small fennel bulbs, halved

4 tomatoes, peeled, seeded, and diced (see Basics)

6 cups (1.5 l) boiling water

2 cups (16 fl oz/500 ml) dry white wine

Bouquet garni: 1 parsley sprig, 1 thyme sprig, and 1 bay leaf,
   tied in a cheesecloth square

8 eggs

8 baguette slices, lightly toasted

2 teaspoons salt

Large pinch of freshly ground black pepper

In a large Dutch oven or flameproof casserole, heat the olive oil over medium heat and sauté the leeks and onions until soft, about 7 minutes. Add the garlic, fennel, tomatoes, water, wine, and bouquet garni. Simmer, uncovered, for 20 to 30 minutes.

Strain into a bowl, pushing the vegetables through with the back of a large spoon. Return the soup to the saucepan and bring to a simmer over medium heat. Season with salt and pepper. Break the eggs, one at a time, into a saucer and slip each into the soup. Poach the eggs for 3 minutes.

Place a baguette slice in each of 8 warmed soup bowls. Using a slotted spoon, top each with a poached egg. Ladle the soup over the egg and bread. Serve at once, with additional bread on the side.

Makes 8 servings

CHEZ TOUTOUNE

Estouffade de Joue de Boeuf, Macaroni au Parmesan

Braised Beef Cheeks with Parmesan Macaroni

A traditional beef stew from the South of France. Although you won't really taste the chocolate in the sauce, it adds a rich, dark flavor to this hearty winter dish.

2 pounds (1 kg) beef cheeks, beef chuck, or lean stewing beef trimmed of all fat and gristle and cut into 2-inch (5-cm) cubes

2 onions, chopped

2 carrots, peeled and chopped

1 garlic clove, minced

12 black peppercorns

1 whole clove

4 juniper berries

Bouquet garni: 1 parsley sprig, 1 thyme sprig, 1 bay leaf, tied in cheesecloth square

1 bottle (750 ml) full-bodied red wine

2 tablespoons peanut oil

¾ cup (6 oz/185 g) butter, cut into small pieces

One ½ ounce (15 g) square unsweetened chocolate, chopped

Salt and freshly ground black pepper to taste

Parmesan Macaroni

1 pound (500 g) elbow macaroni

2 cups (16 oz/500 ml) heavy cream

1 cup (4 oz/125 g) grated Parmesan cheese

Salt and freshly ground black pepper to taste

In a large bowl, combine the beef, onion, carrot, garlic, peppercorns, clove, juniper berries, and bouquet garni. Pour in the red wine, cover the bowl

with plastic wrap, and refrigerate for 24 hours.

Preheat the oven to 300°F (150°C). Using a slotted spoon, transfer the meat to a plate. Transfer the vegetables to a separate plate. Reserve the marinade.

In a large sauté pan or skillet over high heat, heat the peanut oil and brown the meat on all sides. Using a slotted spoon, transfer the meat to a Dutch oven or large casserole.

In the same pan, sauté the vegetables over medium heat until soft, about 5 minutes; transfer to the Dutch oven or casserole. Add the reserved marinade to the sauté pan or skillet, stirring to scrape the browned bits from the bottom of the pan, and simmer for 5 minutes. Pour the liquid into the Dutch oven or casserole and, if necessary, add water to just cover the meat. Cover and bake in the preheated oven, stirring occasionally, for 2 to 3 hours for chuck or stewing beef, 6 hours for beef cheeks, or until the meat is extremely tender.

Using a slotted spoon, transfer the meat to a plate. Strain the sauce through a fine-meshed sieve, pushing the vegetables through with the back of a large spoon, and skim off the fat. Pour the sauce back into the pan and boil until reduced by a third. Reduce heat to low and swirl in the butter and chocolate. Season with salt and pepper. Just before serving, add the meat and heat through.

To make the macaroni: In a large pot of salted boiling water, cook the macaroni until al dente, about 10 minutes; drain. Return the macaroni to the pot. Stir in the cream, Parmesan cheese, salt, and pepper and cook for 5 minutes.

Meanwhile, preheat the broiler. Transfer the macaroni to a gratin dish and place under the preheated broiler just until the cheese is browned and sizzling.

Arrange a portion of stew and macaroni on each plate and serve immediately.

Makes 4 servings

Crème Brûlée à la Fleur d'Oranges

Orange-Flavored Burned Cream

*This silky custard has a crisp sugar topping and is delicately scented
with orange.*

6 large egg yolks

½ cup (4 oz/125 g) sugar

2 cups (16 fl oz/500 ml) heavy cream

2 cups (16 fl oz/500 ml) milk

1 vanilla bean, split lengthwise, or 1 teaspoon vanilla extract

1 handful unsprayed orange blossoms, or 1 tablespoon orange
flower water

8 tablespoons (3½ oz/105 g) firmly packed dark brown sugar

Preheat the oven to 250°F (120°C). In a large bowl, beat the egg yolks and
sugar together until pale.

In a saucepan over medium heat, combine the cream, milk, vanilla
bean, if using, and orange blossoms, if using, and heat over medium heat
until bubbles form around the edges of the pan. Remove from heat, cover,
and set aside to steep for 15 minutes. Strain through a fine-meshed sieve.
Gradually whisk the cream mixture into the egg yolk mixture. Stir in the
vanilla extract and orange flower water, if using.

Place 8 individual ramekins in a baking pan and pour the custard into
the ramekins. Add hot water to the baking pan to come halfway up the
sides of the ramekins. Bake in the preheated oven until the mixture is just
set but still trembling in the center, about 1 hour. Let cool. Refrigerate for
at least 2 hours or up to 24 hours.

Just before serving, preheat the broiler. Place 1 tablespoon of the
brown sugar in a small fine-meshed sieve and push the sugar through with
the back of a spoon to evenly layer the top of a custard. Repeat with the
remaining custards. Place the custards on a baking sheet under the broiler
about 2 inches from the heat source and broil until the sugar is melted and
crisp, about 1 minute; be careful not to burn. Let cool for a few minutes
and serve.

Makes 8 custards

CHEZ TOUTOUNE

CHEZ LA VIEILLE

1, RUE BAILLEUL, 75001 PARIS

MÉTRO PONT-NEUF OR LOUVRE

Hidden away on a quiet street in Paris's bustling tourist-filled first arrondissement is a tiny bistro that serves superb cuisine to local gourmets and a few knowledgeable travelers. Chez la Vieille's first-floor dining room, with its ancient timber-framed walls and stone floor, has just a handful of tables. Upstairs is another small room, but in all only about twenty-five diners can enjoy this bistro at any one time.

Madame Cervoni, the stylish, energetic owner, has added a few specialties from her native Corsica to the menu since 1993 when she took over from Adrienne Biasin, the bistro's founder. But the noteworthy appetizers and menu of classic dishes, such as *boeuf à la mode* and Le Gâteau Froid au Chocolat d'Adrienne (page 220), haven't changed since Madame Biasin first opened her doors in the 1950s. Guests who order the selection of appetizers should be prepared to help themselves from a procession of pâtés, salads, and *charcuterie* brought to the table in large serving dishes. A special treat at Chez la Vieille is the house Kir, an aperitif of white wine with a dash of crème de cassis (black currant liqueur). The cassis, made according to Madame Cervoni's own recipe, adds a unique color and delicious flavor to the drink.

NEIGHBORHOOD WALK

Although Chez la Vieille is located on a quiet corner, the surrounding neighborhood bustles with businesspeople and tourists. And, as is true almost anywhere you walk in Paris, the streets around the bistro are full of delightful surprises: elegant nineteenth-century apartment buildings, a row of pet stores and seed shops, a simple corner bakery, and the sudden appearance of a small cathedral—in this case, St-Germain l'Auxerrois, a former parish church for the royal family at 2, place du Louvre.

Near Chez la Vieille is what was once the largest royal palace in France—the Louvre. By the time of the Revolution, several generations of French monarchs had filled the Louvre's galleries with an extensive collection of important paintings, including Leonardo da Vinci's celebrated Mona Lisa. In 1793, the newly founded French Republic took the hitherto unheard-of step of opening the collections to the public, and the Louvre has been a major destination for art-lovers throughout the world ever since.

The Tuileries gardens, a delightful place for an afternoon stroll, form a narrow green sward between the Louvre and place de la Concorde, the magnificent square originally designed to hold a statue of Louis XV. After the Revolution, the statue was replaced by a guillotine, and the square became a scene of terror where thousands of victims, including Louis XVI, Marie-Antoinette, and Robespierre, were executed. Today, place de la Concorde has become one of the most impressive sites in Paris. Tourists can stand near a three-thousand-year-old Egyptian obelisk in the center of the square, while viewing the Tuileries gardens and the Louvre in one direction and the Champs-Elysées in the other.

Note: If you're interested in purchasing some bistro-style china for your own home, stop at the Verrerie des Halles, just a few minutes away from Chez la Vieille at 15, rue du Louvre. This store, which supplies many Parisian bistros, sells everything from French mustard pots to the perfect little cup and saucer for your morning café au lait.

CHEZ LA VIEILLE

Petits Artichauts Parfumés

Little Perfumed Artichokes

Fricassée de Veau, Légumes et Champignons

Veal Fricassée with Vegetables and Mushrooms

Le Gâteau Froid au Chocolat d'Adrienne

Adrienne's Cold Chocolate Cake

Petits Artichauts Parfumés

Little Perfumed Artichokes

Juice of 2 lemons

4 medium artichokes, quartered, or 12 baby artichokes, halved

⅓ cup (3 fl oz/80 ml) olive oil

24 small white boiling onions

2 garlic cloves, minced

1 pound (500 g) tomatoes, peeled, seeded, and diced (see Basics)

1 celery stalk, chopped

2 fresh thyme sprigs

4 fresh basil leaves, chopped, plus 4 basil leaves, stacked, rolled, and cut crosswise into thin ribbons for garnish

8 black peppercorns

1 teaspoon coriander, coarsely cracked

3 tablespoons balsamic vinegar

Salt and freshly ground black pepper to taste

Fill a large bowl with water and half of the lemon juice. Snap off the tough outer leaves near the bottom of the artichokes and peel the stem, leaving about 1½ inches (4 cm). Slice in half lengthwise and scoop out the chokes with a teaspoon. Add the artichokes to the lemon water to prevent discoloration.

In a large, heavy saucepan over medium heat, heat the olive oil and sauté the onions for about 3 minutes. Add the garlic and sauté for 1 minute. Add the tomatoes, celery, thyme, chopped basil, pepppercorns, coriander, the remaining lemon juice, the vinegar, salt and pepper; simmer for 5 minutes. Add the artichokes, cover the pan tightly, and cook over low heat until the artichokes are tender when pierced by a fork, about 20 minutes. Add a little water if necessary to keep the artichokes moist.

Using a slotted spoon, transfer the artichokes to a deep bowl or casserole dish. Season the sauce with salt and pepper to taste and spoon it over the artichokes. Serve warm or at room temperature, garnished with the sliced basil.

Makes 8 servings

CHEZ LA VIEILLE

Fricassée de Veau, Légumes et Champignons

Veal Fricassée with Vegetables and Mushrooms

⅓ cup (3 fl oz/80 ml) olive oil

4 pounds (2 kg) veal stew meat or shoulder,
 cut into 2-inch (5 cm) cubes

Salt and freshly ground black pepper to taste

1 onion, chopped

2 garlic cloves, chopped

2 tomatoes, chopped

1 fresh basil sprig

1 calf's foot

Bouquet garni: 1 parsley sprig, 1 thyme sprig, 1 bay leaf,
 tied in a cheesecloth square

⅓ cup (3 fl oz/80 ml) dry white wine

Garnish

4 small turnips, peeled and halved

4 small carrots, cut into 2-inch (5-cm) lengths

2 leeks, white parts only, chopped

1 bunch green onion tops, chopped

3½ ounces (105 g) slab bacon or smoked ham, diced

5 tablespoons (2½ oz/75 g) butter

2 shallots, minced

8 ounces (250 g) chanterelle mushrooms, chopped

8 ounces (250 g) oyster mushrooms, chopped

8 ounces (250 g) white mushrooms, chopped

Salt and freshly ground black pepper to taste

In a large, heavy saucepan or Dutch oven over medium heat, heat the olive oil and brown the veal on all sides. Using a slotted spoon, transfer the meat to a plate and season with salt and pepper.

To the same pan, add the onion and garlic and sauté over medium heat for 5 minutes. Stir in the tomatoes, basil, and bouquet garni. Add the calf's foot, veal, wine, and enough water to cover the meat. Raise heat to high and bring to a boil. Reduce heat to low, cover, and simmer gently for 2 hours, or until the meat is extremely tender. Alternatively, the stew may be baked in a preheated 325°F (165°C) oven for 2 hours once it has come to a boil.

Meanwhile, to make the garnish: Separately steam or blanch the turnips, carrots, leeks, and green onion tops until just tender. Set the vegetables aside.

In a large sauté pan or skillet over medium heat, sauté the bacon or ham for 5 minutes (use a little oil to sauté the ham). Add the vegetables and bacon or ham to the pot and stir to combine.

In a sauté pan over medium heat, melt 2 tablespoons of the butter and sauté the shallots until translucent, about 2 minutes. Add all the mushrooms and sauté for 5 minutes. Set aside.

Using a slotted spoon, transfer the veal to a serving dish. Bone the calf's foot and cut the meat into pieces; arrange them and the steamed or blanched vegetables over the veal.

Strain the sauce through a fine-meshed sieve and return it to the saucepan. Bring to a boil, swirl in the remaining 3 tablespoons butter, and season with salt and pepper. Spoon the sauce over the meat and vegetables. Serve the sautéed mushrooms separately as a side dish.

Makes 8 servings

Le Gâteau Froid au Chocolat d'Adrienne

Adrienne's Cold Chocolate Cake

Make this luscious mousse cake a day in advance so the flavors have a chance to blend. Serve with crème anglaise flavored with grated orange zest.

14 ounces (440 g) bittersweet chocolate, chopped

Juice and grated zest of 2 oranges

3 envelopes plain gelatin

1¾ cups (14 oz/440 g) butter at room temperature

8 eggs, separated

⅓ cup (100 g) sugar

¼ teaspoon salt

3 tablespoons slivered blanched almonds

2 cups (16 fl oz/500 ml) crème anglaise (see Basics)

2 teaspoons grated orange zest (see Basics)

In a double boiler over barely simmering water, melt the chocolate. Meanwhile, sprinkle the gelatin over the orange juice and let sit for 5 minutes. Stir the orange juice mixture into the melted chocolate until thoroughly blended. Stir in the butter until melted. Add the orange zest.

In a large bowl, whisk the egg yolks, sugar, and salt together until pale. Gradually stir the egg mixture into the warm chocolate mixture.

In a large bowl, beat the egg whites until stiff, glossy peaks form. Stir one fourth of the whites into the chocolate mixture. Gently fold in the remaining whites until thoroughly blended.

Spread half the almonds over the bottom of a 9-inch (23-cm) springform pan. Pour in the batter and evenly sprinkle the top with the remaining almonds. Cover with plastic wrap and refrigerate for at least 24 hours before serving.

To serve, stir the orange zest into the crème anglaise. Pool some of the crème anglaise on each dessert plate. Seve a wedge of cake on top.

Makes one 9-inch (23-cm) cake; serves 8

BASICS

Applesauce

4 Granny Smith or other tart apples, cored, peeled,
  and cut into wedges

1 cup (8 fl oz/250 ml) water

Juice of ½ lemon

⅓ cup (3 oz/90 g) sugar

½ teaspoon ground cinnamon

In a medium saucepan, combine all the ingredients and cook over medium heat until the apples are tender, about 15 minutes. Using a potato masher, mash the apples and stir until smooth. If you prefer a smoother applesauce, purée in a blender or food processor. Serve warm or at room temperature. Cover and refrigerate to store.

Makes 4 servings

Sautéed Apples

2 tablespoons butter

2 Granny Smith apples, peeled, cored, and quartered

1 tablespoon sugar

In a medium sauté pan or skillet, melt the butter over medium heat. Add the apples, sprinkle with the sugar, and sauté for 15 minutes, or until the apples are very tender and the juice is just beginning to caramelize.

Makes 4 servings

Blanching Bacon

You can remove the salty taste and/or smoky flavor of bacon or salt pork by blanching it. In a small saucepan, combine bacon or salt pork with cold water to cover by 2 or 3 inches (5 or 7.5 cm). Bring to the boil and simmer for 5 to 8 minutes. Drain, rinse under cold water, and pat dry with paper towels.

Clarified Butter

Clarified butter is used for cooking at high temperatures, as it will not burn. In a small, heavy saucepan, melt unsalted butter over low heat. Remove the pan from heat and let stand for several minutes. Skim off the foam and pour off the clear liquid, leaving the milky solids in the bottom of the pan. Cover and store in the refrigerator indefinitely. When clarified, butter loses about one fourth its original volume.

Crème Anglaise

This light custard sauce can be used as a topping or pooled under desserts.

4 egg yolks

½ cup (4 oz/125 g) sugar

1⅓ cups (11 fl oz/330 ml) milk

2 teaspoons vanilla extract

In a medium saucepan, whisk the egg yolks until blended. Gradually whisk in the sugar by spoonfuls. Continue whisking for 2 to 3 minutes, or until the mixture is pale and thick. In a small saucepan, heat the milk over medium-low heat until bubbles form around the edges of the pan. Gradually whisk the hot milk into the egg mixture. Continue to cook, stirring constantly with a wooden spoon, until the sauce thickens enough to coat the spoon. The sauce should gradually come near the simmering point, but do not let it simmer or the yolks will scramble. Stir in the vanilla and let cool. Store, covered, in the refrigerator for 3 or 4 days.

Makes about 1 cup (8 fl oz/250 ml)

Crème Fraîche

Lightly tangy thickened cream is used in sauces and as a topping for both savory and sweet dishes. It can be found in specialty foods stores and some grocery stores. To make crème fraîche at home, mix 2 cups (16 fl oz/500 ml) heavy cream with 2 tablespoons buttermilk in a medium bowl. Cover with plastic wrap and let stand at room temperature overnight or until fairly thick. Refrigerate for at least 4 hours. The cream can be kept in the refrigerator for several days.

Makes 2 cups (16 oz/500 g)

Demi-Glace

Demi-glace, a super-concentrated stock, adds magnificent flavor to sauces, soups, and stews. Preparation from scratch takes hours, but it is available by mail order (see Mail Order Sources).

Roasting Garlic

Roasted garlic is mellower, sweeter, and more subtle in flavor than raw, fresh garlic. Cut off the top of a head of garlic to expose the cloves. Cover the garlic head with aluminum foil and bake in a preheated 350°F (180°C) oven for 30 minutes, or until soft. Squeeze the garlic from the cloves.

Herbes de Provence

When fresh herbs are out of season or hard to find, cooks in the South of France use a traditional mixture of dried herbs that is the essence of the region. Combine 2 tablespoons *each* dried thyme and marjoram with 1 tablespoon *each* dried oregano, summer savory, and rosemary. Mix well and store in a covered jar away from direct sunlight.

Makes about 7 tablespoons (3½ oz)

Ladyfingers
Biscuits à la Cuillère

½ cup (4 oz/125 g) plus 1 tablespoon granulated sugar

3 eggs, separated

1 teaspon vanilla extract

Pinch of salt

⅛ teaspoon cream of tartar

⅔ cup (3 oz/90 g) all-purpose flour

1 cup powdered sugar for sprinkling

Preheat the oven to 300°F (150°C). Butter 2 baking sheets and dust lightly with flour; knock off any excess.

In a large bowl, beat the ½ cup (4 oz/125 g) sugar, the egg yolks, and vanilla together for 2 minutes, or until pale and thick.

In a large bowl, beat the egg whites until foamy. Beat in the salt and cream of tartar until soft peaks form. Sprinkle in the 1 tablespoon granulated sugar and beat until stiff, glossy peaks form. Stir one fourth of the egg whites into the egg yolk mixture. Sprinkle one fourth of the flour over the batter and gently fold in until partially blended. Repeat twice, with half the remaining flour and half the remaining whites each time. Gently fold in the last addition of flour until thoroughly blended; the batter should be light and fluffy.

Using a large spoon or pastry bag, make even lines of batter 4 inches (10 cm) long and 1 inch wide on the prepared baking sheets. Sprinkle each cookie with a layer of powdered sugar. Bake immediately in the preheated oven for 20 minutes, or until the ladyfingers are very pale brown under the sugar coating. Remove from the baking sheet and let cool.

Makes about 25 ladyfingers

Rehydrating Cherries

To rehydrate dried cherries, place in a bowl and cover with hot water. Let soak for 20 minutes, or until soft.

Pastry Cream
Crème Pâtissière

A classic French filling for cakes and pastries.

4 egg yolks

½ cup (4 oz/125 g) sugar

⅓ cup (2 oz/60 g) plus 1 tablespoon all-purpose flour

2 cups (16 fl oz/500 ml) milk

½ vanilla bean, split in half lengthwise, or ½ teaspoon vanilla extract

In a large bowl, whisk the egg yolks and sugar together until pale. Whisk in the flour; set aside.

In a large saucepan over medium heat, bring the milk and vanilla bean, if using, just to a boil; remove from heat. Whisk some of the hot milk into the egg mixture. Return the saucepan to medium heat, and as soon as the mixture comes to a boil, pour in the remaining egg mixture, whisking constantly, until thickened. Return to a boil, stirring constantly. Remove from heat and stir in the vanilla extract, if using. Cover with plastic wrap.

pressing the plastic directly onto the surface of the hot cream to prevent a skin from forming. Let cool completely before using, or store in the refrigerator for 3 or 4 days.

Makes 2¼ cups (18 fl oz/560 ml)

Pâte Brisée
Flaky Pastry

1 cup (5 oz/155 g) all-purpose flour

7 tablespoons (3½ oz/105 g) cold unsalted butter, cut into pieces

⅛ teaspoon salt

3 tablespoons cold water

In a food processor, combine the flour, butter, and salt and process until the mixture resembles coarse crumbs, about 15 seconds. With the motor running, pour in the water in a steady stream and process until the dough begins to form a ball, about 20 seconds. Flatten the dough into a disk, cover with plastic wrap, and refrigerate for at least 45 minutes.

On a lightly floured surface, roll the dough out to a 12-inch (30-cm) circle. Fit into a 10-inch (25-cm) tart pan and trim the edges. Prick the pastry with a fork and refrigerate for 20 minutes. Preheat the oven to 375°F (190°C). Line the shell with aluminum foil and fill with dried beans or pastry weights.

For a partially baked shell: Bake in the preheated oven for 20 minutes, or until lightly colored. Remove the beans or weights and aluminum foil. Prick the bottom of the pstry with a fork and continue baking for 10 minutes, or until lightly browned all over.

For a fully baked shell: Remove the beans or weights and aluminum foil. Prick the pastry with a fork and continue baking for 20 minutes, or until golden brown. Let cool for at least 10 minutes before filling.

Makes one 10-inch (25-cm) partially baked or prebaked pastry shell

Pâte-Demi Feuilletée
Quick Puff Pastry

10 tablespoons (5 oz/150 g) cold unsalted butter

1¼ cups (6½ oz/200 g) all-purpose flour

¼ teaspoon salt

6 to 7 tablespoons cold water

Divide the butter into 4 portions. Sift the flour onto a work surface and make a well in the center. Add 1 portion of the butter, the salt, and 6 tablespoons of the water. Using your fingertips, work together until well mixed. Gradually add the flour until the mixture resembles coarse crumbs. Add the remaining 1 tablespoon water if necessary to moisten all the flour. Press the dough together and pat into a flat disc. Cover with plastic wrap and refrigerate for at least 30 minutes.

On a lightly floured work surface, roll out the dough to a 8-by-14-inch (20-by-35 cm) rectangle. Cut the second portion of butter into small pieces. Sprinkle the butter onto two thirds of the dough. Fold the dough in thirds, folding the nonbuttered third over the center third, then folding over the remaining third of the pastry. Press the ends to seal. Cover with plastic wrap and refrigerate for at least 15 minutes.

Place the dough on the floured work surface with the open edge towards you and roll out into a rectangle. Cut the third portion of butter into small pieces and sprinkle and fold as before. Cover with plastic wrap and refrigerate for at least 15 minutes.

Roll out the dough as above. Cut the fourth portion of butter into small pieces and sprinkle and fold as before. Cover with plastic wrap and refrigerate for up to 3 or 4 days until ready to use.

Makes one 10½-inch (27-cm) shell

Pâte Sablée
Short Pastry

1 cup (5 oz/140 g) all-purpose flour

½ cup (2 oz/60 g) powdered sugar

6 tablespoons (3 oz/90 g) butter at room temperature

⅛ teaspoon salt

1 egg, lightly beaten

In a food processor, combine the flour, sugar, butter, and salt and process until the mixture resembles coarse crumbs, about 15 seconds. With the motor running, pour in the water in a steady stream and process until the dough begins to form a ball, about 20 seconds. Flatten the dough into a disk.

Using your fingers, quickly press the dough into a 10-inch (25 cm) tart pan. Cover the shell with plastic wrap and refrigerate for at least 2 hours.

Preheat the oven to 375°F (190°C). Line the shell with aluminum foil and fill with dried beans or pastry weights.

For a partially baked shell: Bake in the preheated oven for 20 minutes. Remove the beans or weights and aluminum foil. Prick the bottom of the shell with a fork and continue baking for 10 minutes, or until lightly browned all over.

For a fully baked shell: Remove the beans or weights and aluminum foil. Prick the bottom of the shell with a fork and continue baking for 20 minutes, or until golden brown. Let cool before filling.

Makes one 10-inch (25-cm) partially baked or prebaked pastry shell

Pâte Sucrée
Sweet Pastry

1 cup (5 oz/140 g) all-purpose flour

7 tablespoons (3½ oz/105 g) butter, chilled and cut into pieces

2 tablespoons sugar

⅛ teaspoon salt

3 tablespoons water

In a food processor, add the flour, butter, sugar, and salt and process until the mixture resembles coarse crumbs, about 15 seconds. With the motor running, pour in the water in a steady stream and process until the dough begins to form a ball, about 20 seconds. Flatten the dough into a disk, cover with plastic wrap, and refrigerate for at least 45 minutes.

On a lightly floured surface, roll the dough out to a 12-inch (30-cm) circle. Fit into a 10-inch (25-cm) tart pan and trim the edges. Prick the pastry with a fork and refrigerate for 20 minutes. Preheat the oven to 375°F (190°C). Line the shell with aluminum foil and fill with dried beans or pastry weights.

For a partially baked shell: Bake in the preheated oven for 20 minutes. Remove the beans or weights and aluminum foil. Prick the bottom of the shell with a fork and continue baking for 10 minutes, or until lightly browned all over.

For a fully baked shell: Remove the beans or weights and aluminum foil. Prick the bottom of the pastry shell with a fork and continue baking for 20 minutes. Let cool before filling.

Makes one 10-inch (25-cm) partially baked or prebaked pastry shell

Peeling and Seeding Tomatoes

Cut out the cores of the tomatoes and cut an X in the opposite end. Drop the tomatoes into a pot of rapidly boiling water for 10 seconds, or until the skin by the X peels away slightly. Drain and run cold water over the tomatoes; the skin should slip off easily. To seed, cut the tomatoes in half crosswise, hold each half upside down over the sink, and gently squeeze and shake to remove the seeds.

Rendering Duck or Goose Fat

Preheat the oven to 350°F (180°C). Cut duck or goose skin and fat into ¼-inch-wide (6-mm) strips. Arrange the strips in a baking dish and bake in the preheated oven, tossing occasionally, for 30 minutes, or until browned. Strain the clear yellow fat from the cracklings into a jar. Cover and refrigerate for up to several weeks.

Place the fat in a heavy pot. Cook over low heat until all the fat liquifies; this could take an hour or more, depending on the amount of fat. Strain the clear fat through a fine-meshed sieve. Let cool and refrigerate until ready to use.

To Section Citrus Fruit

Cut off the top and bottom of an orange, grapefruit, lime, or lemon down to the flesh, then stand the fruit upright and cut off the peel in sections down to the flesh. Working over a bowl to catch the juice, hold the fruit in one hand and cut between the membranes. Rotate the fruit and let the section fall into the bowl. Pick out any seeds.

Simple Syrup

In a small, heavy saucepan, combine 1 cup (8 oz/250 g) sugar and ⅓ cup (3 fl oz/80 ml) water. Bring to a simmer over medium heat. Cook until the sugar has dissolved. Remove from heat and let cool. Pour into an airtight container. Cover and store in the refrigerator for up to 6 months.

Makes about 1 cup (8 fl oz/250 ml)

Superfine Sugar

Superfine sugar can be found in most grocery stores, but it can be made easily by blending regular granulated sugar in a blender or food processor to a finer consistency.

Toasting Walnuts

Preheat the oven to 350°F (180°C). Spread the nuts on a baking sheet and bake for 10 to 15 minutes, or until fragrant and very lightly browned, stirring once or twice.

Vinaigrette

4 tablespoons (2 fl oz/60 ml) red wine vinegar

1 teaspoon salt

¼ teaspoon freshly ground black pepper

⅔ cup (5 fl oz/150 ml) canola oil or extra-virgin olive oil

In a small bowl, whisk the vinegar, salt, and pepper together. Gradually whisk in the olive oil in a slow, steady stream until emulsified.

Makes about 1 cup (8 fl oz/250 ml)

Dijon Vinaigrette

1 tablespoon (1 oz/30 g) Dijon mustard

⅓ cup (3 fl oz/90 g) red wine vinegar

1 cup (8 fl oz/250 ml) canola oil

Salt and ground white pepper to taste

In a small bowl, whisk the mustard, vinegar, salt, and pepper together. Gradually whisk in the canola oil until emulsified.

Makes about 1⅓ cups

Lemon and Orange Zest

To make strips: Using a vegetable peeler or sharp paring knife, cut thin strips of the colored part (the zest) of the lemon or orange peel; don't include the white pith underneath, which is bitter.

To grate: Use a zester or grater to remove the zest of the lemon or orange, or cut strips of zest into very fine pieces with a large knife.

STOCKS

Beef Stock

4 pounds (2 kg) meaty sliced beef shanks

2 tablespoons olive oil

1 onion, chopped

1 carrot, peeled and chopped

1 celery stalk, chopped

1 bay leaf

3 fresh flat-leaf parsley sprigs

6 black peppercorns

½ cup (4 fl oz/125 ml) dry white wine

3 quarts (3 l) water

½ cup (4 fl oz/125 ml) tomato purée

Salt and freshly ground black pepper to taste

Preheat the oven to 400°F (200°C). In a roasting pan, toss the bones with the olive oil. Brown for 30 to 40 minutes, turning occasionally. Transfer the bones to a large saucepan or kettle.

Pour the fat out of the roasting pan. Place the pan over medium heat, add the wine, and stir to scrape up the browned bits from the bottom of the pan. Pour this liquid into the saucepan or kettle with the remaining ingredients. Bring to a boil and skim off any foam that rises to the top. Simmer slowly for 3 to 4 hours, or until the stock is well flavored.

Strain through a sieve into a bowl and let cool. Refrigerate until cold. Remove the congealed fat on the surface. Store in the refrigerator for up to 3 days. To keep longer, bring to a boil every 3 days or freeze for up to 3 months.

Makes about 1 quart

Chicken Stock
Fond de Volaille

2 onions, coarsely chopped

Bouquet garni: 4 parsley sprigs, 4 peppercorns, 1 thyme sprig, and 1 bay leaf, tied in a cheesecloth square

4 pounds (2 kg) chicken pieces such as backs, necks, and wings

2 carrots, peeled and chopped

3 celery stalks, chopped

5 garlic cloves

In a stockpot, combine all the ingredients and add water to cover by 2 inches (5 cm). Bring to a boil and skim off any foam that forms on the surface. Reduce heat to low and simmer, uncovered, for 1 1/2 to 2 hours, or until the stock is well flavored. Strain through a fine-meshed sieve into a clean container. Let cool, cover, and refrigerate until cold. Remove the congealed fat from the surface. Store in the refrigerator for up to 3 days. To keep longer, bring to a boil every 3 days, or freeze for up to 3 months.

Makes about 2½ quarts (2.5 l)

Rich Chicken and Beef Stock

5½ (2.75 kg) pounds chicken wings and backs

3 pounds (1.5 kg) beef short ribs, cut into 3-inch (7.5-cm) pieces

6 carrots, peeled and cut into 3-inch (7.5-cm) pieces

4 turnips, peeled and quartered

4 leeks, split lengthwise and rinsed well

2 celery stalks, halved lengthwise

1 large onion, quartered

2 fresh thyme sprigs

1 bay leaf

1 teaspoon whole black peppercorns

1 bunch fresh parsley stems, tied with string

5 quarts (5 l) water

In a large stockpot, combine all the ingredients and bring to a boil. Reduce heat to low and simmer for 4 hours, skimming any foam that rises to the surface. Let cool.

Strain the stock through a fine-meshed sieve into a large saucepan. Simmer briskly over medium heat until well flavored. Let cool, cover, and refrigerate until cold. Remove the congealed fat from the surface. Store in the refrigerator for up to 3 days. To keep longer, bring to a boil every 3 days, or freeze for up to 3 months.

Fish Stock
Fumet de Poisson

4 pounds (2 kg) heads and bones of white-fleshed fish such as sole or whiting, cut up

2 quarts (2 l) water

1 carrot, sliced

2 onions, chopped

1 celery stalk, sliced

Bouquet garni: 6 parsley stems, 4 peppercorns, 1 fresh thyme sprig, and 1 bay leaf, tied in a cheesecloth square

1 cup (8 fl oz/250 ml) dry white wine

In a stockpot, combine the fish heads, bones, and water. Bring to a boil, skimming off the scum that rises to the surface. Reduce heat to low, add the remaining ingredients, and simmer for 30 minutes. Remove from heat and strain through a sieve into a large saucepan. Bring to a boil and cook to reduce the liquid by about one third. Use immediately, or let cool, cover, and refrigerate for up to 3 days. To keep longer, bring to a boil every 3 days, or freeze for up to 3 months.

Veal Stock
Fond de Veau

4 pounds (2 kg) veal bones

2 onions

4 cloves

1 carrot, peeled and chopped

2 celery stalks, chopped

3 garlic cloves

⅓ cup (5 fl oz/150 ml) tomato paste

Bouquet garni: 4 parsley sprigs, 2 peppercorns, 1 thyme sprig, and 1 bay leaf, tied in a cheesecloth square

½ cup (4 fl oz/125 ml) dry white wine or water

BASICS

Preheat the oven to 500°F (260°C). Arrange the veal bones in a baking pan and bake for 20 minutes.

Chop one of the onions and stud the other with the cloves. Remove the pan from the oven and arrange the onion, carrot, celery, garlic, and tomato paste evenly over the bones. Return to the oven and bake until the vegetables are lightly browned, about 20 minutes.

Using a slotted spoon, transfer all the solid ingredients to a stockpot. Add the bouquet garni. Pour off the fat from the baking pan and place the pan over medium heat. Pour in the wine or water and stir to scrape up the browned bits from the bottom of the pan. Pour the liquid into the stockpot.

Add water to cover the ingredients by 2 inches (5 cm). Bring to a boil and skim off any foam that rises to the surface. Reduce heat to low and simmer for about 3 hours. Strain the stock through a fine-meshed sieve into a clean container. Let cool, cover, and refrigerate until cold. Remove the congealed fat from the top. Store in the refrigerator for up to 3 days. To keep longer, bring to a boil every 3 days, or freeze for up to 3 months.

Makes about 3½ quarts (3.5 l)

Reduced Stock or Broth

Cook unsalted stock or broth at a low boil until reduced by about one third, or until richly flavored.

CONVERSION CHARTS

Weight Measurements

Standard U.S.	Ounces	Metric
1 ounce	1	30 g
¼ pound (4 ounces)	4	125 g
½ pound (8 ounces)	8	250 g
1 pound	16	500 g
1½ pounds	24	750 g
2 pounds	32	1 kg
2½ pounds	40	1.25 kg
3 pounds	48	1.5 kg

Volume Measurements

Standard U.S.	Fluid Ounces	Metric
1 tablespoon	½	15 ml
2 tablespoons	1	30 ml
3 tablespoons	1½	45 ml
¼ cup (4 tablespoons)	2	60 ml
6 tablespoons	3	90 ml
½ cup (8 tablespoons)	4	125 ml
1 cup	8	250 ml
1 pint (2 cups)	16	500 ml
4 cups	32	1 l

Oven Temperatures

Fahrenheit	Celsius	Gas Mark
250°	120°	½
275°	135°	1
300°	150°	2
325°	165°	3
350°	180°	4
375°	190°	5
400°	200°	6
425°	220°	7

Note: For ease of use, measurements have been rounded off.

Conversion Factors

Ounces to grams: Multiply the ounce figure by 28.3 to get the number of grams.

Pounds to grams: Multiply the pound figure by 453.59 to get the number of grams.

Pounds to kilograms: Multiply the pound figure by 0.45 to get the number of kilograms.

Ounces to milliliters: Multiply the ounce figure by 30 to get the number of milliliters.

Cups to liters: Multiply the cup figure by 0.24 to get the number of liters.

Fahrenheit to Celsius: Subtract 32 from the Fahrenheit figure, multiply by 5, then divide by 9 to get the Celsius figure.

CONVERSION CHARTS

CONTRIBUTORS

Chez Allard
41, rue St-André-des-Arts
75006 Paris
Tel: (33) 01.43.26.48.23
Métro: St-Michel or Odéon

Astier
44, rue Jean-Pierre-Timbaud
75011 Paris
Tel: (33) 01.43.57.16.35
Métro: Parmentier

Auberge Pyrénées-Cévennes
106, rue de la Folie-Méricourt
75011 Paris
Tel: (33) 01.43.57.33.78
Métro: République

Balthazar
80 Spring Street
New York, NY 10012
Tel: (212) 965-1414

Bouchon
6534 Washington Street
Yountville, CA 94599
Tel: (707) 944-8037

La Cagouille
10, place Brancusi
75014 Paris
Tel: (33) 01.43.22.09.01
Métro: Gaîté

Chez Diane
25, rue Servandoni
75006 Paris
Tel: (33) 01.46.33.12.06
Métro: St-Sulpice

La Fontaine de Mars
129, rue St-Dominique
75007 Paris
Tel: (33) 01.47.05.46.44
Métro: Ecole Militaire

La Gargote
351, Place d'Youville
H2Y 2B7 Montréal, Québec
Tel: (514) 844-1428

Chez Germaine
30, rue Pierre-Leroux
75007 Paris
Tel: (33) 01.42.73.28.34
Métro: Vaneau or Duroc

La Grille
80, rue du Faubourg-Poissonnière
75010 Paris
Tel: (33) 01.47.70.89.73
Métro: Poissonnière

Le Grizzli
7, rue St-Martin
75004 Paris
Tel: (33) 01.48.87.77.56
Métro: Hôtel-de-Ville or Châtelet

Restaurant Marie-Louise
52, rue Championnet
75018 Paris
Tel: (33) 01.46.06.86.55
Métro: Simplon or Porte-de-
Clignancourt

Chez Pauline
5, rue Villedo
75001 Paris
Tel: (33) 01.42.96.20.70
Métro: Pyramides

Le Petit Marguery
9, boulevard de Port-Royal
75013 Paris
Tel: (33) 01.43.31.58.59
Métro: Gobelins

Au Pied de Fouet
45, rue de Babylone
75007 Paris
Tel: (33) 01.47.05.12.27
Métro: Vaneau or St-François-
Xavier

Polidor
41, rue Monsieur-le-Prince
75006 Paris
Tel: (33) 01.43.26.95.34
Métro: Odéon, Cluny, or
Luxembourg

La Poule au Pot
9, rue Vauvilliers
75001 Paris
Tel: (33) 01.42.36.32.96
Métro: Louvre or Les Halles

Chez Toutoune
5, rue de Pontoise
75005 Paris
Tel: (33) 01.43.26.56.81
Métro: Maubert-Mutualité

Chez La Vieille
1, rue Bailleul
75001 Paris
Tel: (33) 01.42.60.15.78
Métro: Pont-Neuf or Louvre

CONTRIBUTORS

Mail Order Sources

Balducci's
424 Avenue of the Americas
New York, NY 10011
(800) 822-1444
(212) 673-2600
www.balducci.com

Cheeses, foie gras, truffles, vinegars, oils, and charcuterie; overnight delivery.

D'Artagnan
280 Wilson Avenue
Newark, NJ 07105
(800) 327-8246
(973) 344-0565
www.dartagnan.com

Foreign and domestic foie gras, confit of goose or duck, goose and duck fat, fresh duck, dried and fresh (in season) mushrooms; overnight delivery.

Dean & Deluca
Catalog Center
2526 East 36th Street North Circle
Wichita, KS 67219
(316) 838-1255
(800) 221-7714
www.dean-deluca.com

Smoked goose, foie gras, truffles, oils, vinegars, and French cheeses; overnight delivery.

Sur La Table
Catalog Division
1765 Sixth Avenue South
Seattle, WA 98134
(800) 243-0852
(206) 682-7175

A selection of basic tools and equipment as well as an assortment of hard-to-find specialty items for cooking and baking.

Williams-Sonoma
10,000 Covington Cross
Las Vegas, NV 89134
(800) 542-2233
www.williams-sonoma.com

A wide variety of supplies such as bistro-style dinnerware, glassware, table linens, and flatware; terrines and ramekins; and some specialty foods.

Ideal Cheese Shop, Ltd.
1205 Second Avenue
New York, NY 10021
(800) 382-0109
(212) 688-7579
www.idealcheese.com

Domestic and imported cheeses delivered throughout the United States.

ACKNOWLEDGEMENTS

I would like to thank the many people who made this volume possible.

My deepest gratitude to the proprietors and chefs of the bistros who generously contributed their recipes to the cookbook: Robert Allard and Michel Vola of Chez Allard; Monsieur Clerc and Monsieur Vergnaud of Astier; Daniel and Françoise Constantin of Auberge Pyrénées-Cévennes; Keith McNally, Michael LaHara, Riad Nasr, and Lee Hanson of Balthazar; Thomas Keller, Joseph Keller, Joseph Schwartz, and Shuna Lydon of Bouchon; Gerard Allemandou of La Cagouille; Monsieur and Madame Derrieux of Chez Diane; Christiane Boudon of La Fontaine de Mars; Jean-Pierre Ousset of La Gargote; Ingrid Blakeley of Chez Germaine; Geneviève and Yves Cullère of Restaurant de la Grille; Bernard AIf of Le Grizzli; Guy Roussel and Yves Clémenceau of Restaurant Marie-Louise; André Génin of Chez Pauline; Alain, Jacques, and Michel Cousin of Le Petit Marguery; Monsieur Chich of Au Pied de Fouet; André Maillet of Polidor; Paul Racat of La Poule au Pot; Colette Dejean of Chez Toutoune; Madame Cervoni of Chez la Vieille.

I am forever grateful to clarinetist Ken Peplowski for making this recording a dream come true. Affectionate thanks to violinist Federico Ruiz, guitarist Frank Vignola, guitarist Mike Peters, bassist Michael Moore, accordionist Charlie Giordano, and clarinetist Ken Peplowski for their brilliant performances. Thank you, Malcolm Addey, assisted by Scott Young, for the excellent recording done at Avatar Studios, New York City. Thanks to Forrests Music, Ifshin Violins, Dale Sheets, Glen Barros, and Julie M. Hiryak.

My most sincere thanks to Paul Moore for his stunning photographs, Amy Nathan for her beautiful food styling, and Sara Slavin for her gorgeous tableware.

I want to especially thank Sarah Creider, who was central to this whole endeavor; thank you for your many contributions, the great times together in Paris, the translations, and all of your assistance during the past two years.

Once again, deep gratitude to my longtime editor Carolyn Miller for her expert advice, editorial guidance, and attention to detail. Thanks to Brent Beck of Fifth Street Design for his wonderful book and cover design and enthusiastic support of this project. Molly Stevens, from The Art of Translation, New York City, deserves acknowledgment for her assistance. Thanks to George Young for all his sage advice. I also owe many thanks to Sharlene Swacke, Connie Woods, Ned Waring, the newly married Tim Forney, Mike Coykendall, and all of the staff at Menus and Music.

And as always, to my daughters, Claire and Caitlin, and my husband, John, for their adventurous appetites and their love.

ACKNOWLEDGEMENTS

INDEX

Following French style, any articles such as *au*, *la*, or *le* and the word *chez* appearing before the proper name of an establishment are ignored in the alphabetizing. For example, Au Pied de Fouet is listed as "Pied de Fouet, Au" and Chez Pauline is listed as "Pauline, Chez," both under the letter P.